CONOR McPHERSON

Conor McPherson was born in Dublin in 1971. His original
plays include *The Seafarer* (National Theatre and Broadway;
Tony Award nominations for Best Play and Best Director;
Laurence Olivier and Evening Standard Award nominations for
Best Play), *Shining City* (Royal Court Theatre, London, and
Broadway; Tony Award nomination for Best Play), *Port
Authority* (New Ambassadors, London; Gate Theatre, Dublin;
Atlantic Theatre, New York), *Dublin Carol* (Royal Court; Gate
Theatre; Atlantic Theatre), *The Weir* (Royal Court and
Broadway; Laurence Olivier Award for Best New Play), *St
Nicholas* (Bush Theatre, London), *This Lime Tree Bower* (Bush
Theatre), *The Good Thief* (Dublin Theatre Festival), *Rum and
Vodka* (Fly by Night Theatre Co., Dublin). His adaptations
include *The Birds* (Gate Theatre, Dublin). Further awards for
his work in theatre and cinema include the Evening Standard
Award, Critics' Circle Award, George Devine Award, Meyer-
Whitworth Award, Stewart Parker Award, three Irish Film and
Television Academy Best Screenplay Awards, the Méliès
d'Argent Award for Best European Film (*The Eclipse*), the
CICAE Award for Best Film Berlin Film Festival (*Saltwater*),
the Spanish Circle of Screenwriters Award for Best Screenplay
and the San Sebastian Award for Best Film (*I Went Down*).

Conor McPherson

THE VEIL

NICK HERN BOOKS

London

www.nickhernbooks.co.uk

A Nick Hern Book

The Veil first published in Great Britain as a paperback original in 2011 by Nick Hern Books Limited, 14 Larden Road, London W3 7ST

The Veil copyright © 2011 Conor McPherson

Conor McPherson has asserted his right to be identified as the author of this work

Cover photograph: Emily Taaffe by Dean Rogers
Cover design: Ned Hoste 2H

Typeset by Nick Hern Books
Printed in Great Britain by CPI Group (UK) Ltd, Croydon, CR0 4YY

A CIP catalogue record for this book is available from the British Library

ISBN   978 1 84842 202 5

For Fionnuala and Sumati

The Veil was first performed in the Lyttelton auditorium of the National Theatre, London, on 4 October 2011 (previews from 27 September), with the following cast:

MRS GOULDING	Bríd Brennan
CLARE WALLACE	Caoilfhionn Dunne
MARIA LAMBROKE	Ursula Jones
MR FINGAL	Peter McDonald
REVEREND BERKELEY	Jim Norton
CHARLES AUDELLE	Adrian Schiller
HANNAH LAMBROKE	Emily Taaffe
MADELEINE LAMBROKE	Fenella Woolgar
Director	Conor McPherson
Designer	Rae Smith
Lighting Designer	Neil Austin
Sound Designer	Paul Arditti
Music	Stephen Warbeck

Characters

LADY MADELEINE LAMBROKE, *a widow*
HANNAH LAMBROKE, *her daughter*
MARIA LAMBROKE, *known as 'Grandie', Madeleine's*
    grandmother
THE REVEREND BERKELEY, *a defrocked Anglican minister*
MR CHARLES AUDELLE, *a philosopher*
MRS GOULDING, *a housekeeper and nurse*
MR FINGAL, *an estate manager*
CLARE WALLACE, *a housemaid*

Setting: A fine old house in the Irish Countryside.

Time: Early summer, 1822.

This text went to press before the end of rehearsals and so may differ slightly from the play as performed.

ACT ONE

*Evening of Wednesday May 15th, 1822. Late in the evening –
after 11 p.m.*

*The spacious drawing room of a big house in the countryside in
Ireland. The room is gloomily lit by one or two candles. There
are large windows, beyond which are mature trees with rich
foliage, but for now they are unseen in the darkness. Heavy
raindrops are heard falling out in the night.*

*There is a mantelpiece, stage right, with a large mirror above it.
Some dark old portraits and landscapes grace the walls. The
effect should be that the house has seen better days and needs
some care. This room was once a versatile social space for
receptions and dancing, now it looks bare. What chairs are here
are lined against the walls, the only exceptions being one near
the fireplace and one near a piano.*

*Among the entrances are a main door to the hallway, stage left,
and high double doors in the back wall, leading to a
conservatory with steps to the garden.*

A man, MR FINGAL, *stands in the room, perhaps peering out
the window, lost in thought. He wears dirty boots and a shabby-
looking coat which is wet and torn. An old horse blanket is
draped round his shoulders. While he may be younger, he looks
at least forty. He is broad-shouldered and strong but looks tired.
He hears a door slam out in the hallway and looks up. Light
spills in as* MRS GOULDING *approaches, carrying a lamp and
a bucket. She stops in the doorway. She is about sixty, small and
wiry with a lined, intelligent face.*

MRS GOULDING. Mr Fingal!

FINGAL. Mrs Goulding.

MRS GOULDING. I might have known it was your muddy boots!

FINGAL. What?

MRS GOULDING. You have dirt and mud and whatever else all across the floor out here.

FINGAL. Oh, I'm sorry.

MRS GOULDING. What way did you come up?

FINGAL. I came up through the scullery.

MRS GOULDING. The scullery!

FINGAL. Clare let me in…

MRS GOULDING. I don't believe this! Could you not look at what you were doing?

FINGAL. I couldn't see! Sure there's hardly a candle lit in the place!

MRS GOULDING. Do not dare rebuke me, sir! Where have you been?

FINGAL. I was abroad – almost up as far as Queensfort! – looking for Miss Hannah.

MRS GOULDING. Yes, well, her ladyship found her herself.

MRS GOULDING *crosses to the coal scuttle near the fireplace and, using a rag, takes some pieces of coal, which she puts in her bucket.*

FINGAL. Where was she?

MRS GOULDING. Down in the glen. We're heating water for her bath.

FINGAL. What happened?

MRS GOULDING. I don't know. They had an argument.

FINGAL. Were you not here?

MRS GOULDING. No. I had the evening off.

FINGAL. Well, that's nice…

MRS GOULDING. I had the evening off to go to my niece's house. Nearly every child in the parish has scarlet fever, and her baby got it.

FINGAL (*chastened*). Oh, well…

MRS GOULDING. Yah. We were waiting for a woman from Clonturk who was supposed to have the cure. She arrived full of poitín and nearly fell into the fire, the bloody tinker.

FINGAL. How is the child?

MRS GOULDING. My niece's child?

FINGAL. Yes.

MRS GOULDING. She won't last the night. (*Wipes her hands.*) Where's the boy? We need turf brought in.

FINGAL. I sent him home. I'll bring turf in.

MRS GOULDING. No, I'll get it. We were heating some stew for Miss Hannah. It'll be nearly warm if you want.

FINGAL. I'm alright. I'm just waiting for her ladyship.

MRS GOULDING. You can give me those boots now.

She pulls the horse blanket from his shoulders and throws it on the floor.

FINGAL. Hah?

MRS GOULDING. Stand on that. Here.

She moves a chair for him to sit on. He starts to unlace his boots.

I'll kill that young one for letting you walk all up here like that.

FINGAL. It wasn't her fault.

MRS GOULDING. Not a brain between yous.

FINGAL. It was dark, she didn't see.

MRS GOULDING. I'll rip her bloody ear off for her. (*Tugs at his torn sleeve*.) Where's your good coat?

FINGAL. It got wet in the rain.

MRS GOULDING. You didn't lose it playing cards down in Jamestown, no?

FINGAL. No.

MRS GOULDING. No?

FINGAL. No!

MRS GOULDING. You were always a bad liar, Mr Fingal. Which is why you shouldn't play cards.

FINGAL. Yes, well, I don't.

MRS GOULDING. Yah, right you don't. Down in that kip. With them animals. Sure look at you! You're not able for them, man. The dark rings under your eyes. What are we going to do with you? And no good coat to present yourself tomorrow.

FINGAL. What's tomorrow?

MRS GOULDING. Thursday.

FINGAL. I know what day it is. I mean why do I have to present myself?

MRS GOULDING. Has no one told you?

FINGAL. No.

MRS GOULDING. Her ladyship's cousin, the Reverend Berkeley, is arriving from London.

FINGAL. What!

MRS GOULDING. He's bringing a companion and they'll want to go grousing, I've no doubt, so you better see about them horses. Madam is fit to be tied – both horses lame and she going out to look for Miss Hannah earlier.

FINGAL. The both of them?

MRS GOULDING. They're both lame. Mike Wallace had to hitch up his old grey mare to the buggy and she could hardly pull it! Madam is not the least bit happy, I can tell you. And listen, we'll need to stir a churn of milk out of somewhere for tomorrow.

She takes up his boots.

FINGAL. Why?

MRS GOULDING. Because the cows are all huddled up the far end of the field under the trees and won't be shifted. (*Indicates the rifle.*) What's that rifle doing in here?

FINGAL. Some young lads were throwing stones at us earlier.

MADELEINE LAMBROKE, *the lady of the house, appears at the door to the hallway. She is in her early forties. She is attractive and sombrely dressed. She looks worn out from worry.* MRS GOULDING *looks at her.*

MRS GOULDING. I'll have your boots down at the door. I'll give you a can of stew for the boy's supper on the way out.

FINGAL. Thank you.

MRS GOULDING. Madam.

MADELEINE. Thank you, Mrs Goulding.

MRS GOULDING. Yes, madam.

MRS GOULDING *leaves, taking the boots and bucket with her.* MADELEINE *and* FINGAL *stand there for a moment.*

FINGAL. I trust Miss Hannah is alright.

MADELEINE. Yes, thank you.

FINGAL. We went looking for her up towards Queensfort. There are some new foals up there. I thought she might have gone for a look.

MADELEINE. No. She was sitting down by the brook in the glen. A place her father used to take her.

FINGAL. I see.

MADELEINE. Well, thank you for looking.

FINGAL. Of course.

Pause.

MADELEINE. Well?

FINGAL (*producing some coins*). Of the householders I could find and speak to, four holdings have paid quarterlies. Thirty-seven have withheld all payment.

MADELEINE. Thirty-seven?

FINGAL. They have organised themselves into one body formally requesting they might delay payment until their crops are renewed in the autumn.

MADELEINE. And you have accepted these terms?

FINGAL. I have accepted nothing. If you agree, I will go to the magistrate in the morning. Perhaps he could have a constable down here by the end of the week.

MADELEINE. Huh! That's exactly what happened before and here we are again.

FINGAL. They have not the means, madam.

MADELEINE. Yes, well, neither do I! Think how different it would be if there was a man in charge here.

FINGAL *looks down.*

Water is pouring in the gable end of the upstairs landing.

FINGAL. I will take a look at first light.

MADELEINE. It needs a roofer, Mr Fingal.

FINGAL. Yes, madam.

MADELEINE. Did you call on Colonel Bennett?

FINGAL. Yes, madam. He is happy to extend further credit if and when your estate should require. (*Short pause*.) We could ask him to talk to the magistrate on our behalf, should you wish.

MADELEINE. We better not. His wife can barely withstand the attention the Colonel pays us here yet.

FINGAL. His groundsman told me that even the Colonel may be forced to half his rents to avoid a mass eviction. There's talk of more soldiers being garrisoned at Queensfort and the Colonel's thinking is that we hold fast now and hopefully when the crops are renewed, or when the public works commence...

MADELEINE. Yes, well...

FINGAL. He has also... reiterated his offer to buy the houses you own in Jamestown.

MADELEINE. Yes...

FINGAL. And he has suggested again he is willing to make an offer for portions of the entire estate if...

MADELEINE (*impatiently*). Yes, I am well aware of the Colonel's addiction to acquiring property. Look, the reason I wanted to see you, Mr Fingal...

FINGAL. You received my letter...

MADELEINE. Yes, I received your letter, but that is not the reason I wanted to see you.

She holds an unopened letter to him.

FINGAL. You have not opened it.

MADELEINE. No I have not. Is it of a personal nature? (*Pause*.) Is it of a personal nature?

Pause. He takes it.

FINGAL. Yes.

MADELEINE. Then I will not read it. I want no more of these letters, Mr Fingal. While I appreciate your offers of… friendship, understand that such is impossible. I cannot reciprocate on any level. My status as a widow is one I bear without regret. Entirely.

FINGAL. Yes, madam.

MADELEINE. So kindly desist. While matters remain cordial.

FINGAL. Yes, madam.

MADELEINE. But thank you.

FINGAL. Yes, madam.

MADELEINE. The reason I wanted to see you is that my cousin, the Reverend Berkeley, arrives here from London tomorrow. He will accompany Hannah to Northamptonshire where she will be married in six weeks' time.

FINGAL. Married?

MADELEINE. Yes. (*Short pause.*) Her fiancé is the Marquis of Newbury, the eldest son of Lord Ashby, whose seat is outside Northampton.

FINGAL. I see.

MADELEINE. My cousin being a trusted spiritual advisor to Lord Ashby, has kindly agreed to chaperone Hannah to Northampton while I settle my affairs here. These matters have been undertaken with great delicacy and as such I have not been at liberty to disclose anything to you or the household before now.

FINGAL. I understand.

MADELEINE. It is my intention to travel to England for the wedding.

FINGAL. Of course.

MADELEINE. And I will remain there.

Short pause.

FINGAL. For how long?

MADELEINE. Indefinitely.

FINGAL. I see.

MADELEINE. I am mindful you have not received your salary for…?

FINGAL. Thirteen months, madam.

MADELEINE. Yes. Well, Hannah's forthcoming union will release a good deal of revenue towards this estate and all outstanding debts will be satisfied.

FINGAL. Thank you, madam.

MADELEINE. Despite the problems we have been beset with here, Mr Fingal, I hope you will remain as estate manager in my absence. Things have been run tolerably well and I expect may be maintained to a satisfactory degree under your charge.

FINGAL. Yes, madam.

MADELEINE. While I have been advised to sell the estate, and indeed I may have to, I am disinclined at present. This is our home. I regard those we know here as our friends.

FINGAL. Of course.

MADELEINE. I know how all of this must appear disruptive, Mr Fingal…

FINGAL. No…

MADELEINE. But one must act in the interests of the estate.

FINGAL. Naturally.

MADELEINE. And Hannah's best interests obviously.

FINGAL. Obviously. You will forgive me for seeming forward... but I had heard...

MADELEINE (*softens towards him*). Heard what?

FINGAL. That Miss Hannah was... That an old complaint had... returned.

MADELEINE. Who told you?

FINGAL. Only those that are within the house.

MADELEINE. Who? Clare? (*Pause.*) Yes well, I'm sure half of Jamestown knows so you may as well tell me. What have you heard?

FINGAL. I have heard that Miss Hannah says she has been hearing voices here again.

Pause.

MADELEINE. Yes, well, so she says.

FINGAL. Do you think this is an appropriate time for her to be married?

MADELEINE. You are too forward, Mr Fingal.

FINGAL. Yes, madam.

MADELEINE (*dismissively*). She used to always claim that while she played the piano, she could hear someone... singing. Or crying. I forget which. She always said that.

FINGAL. Yes, I remember.

MADELEINE (*playing it down*). So... (*Pause. Considers him, unable to stop herself from opening up.*) Now she says she heard some man shouting in here on Sunday evening. She ran down to the kitchen and sat with Clare until I came back from the Colonel's dinner. You weren't calling out to the boy outside or...?

FINGAL. On Sunday we had our dinner in Jamestown. There was no noise or shouting here to my knowledge. I mean, it might have been...

MADELEINE (*interrupting him*). Yes, well, I am sure there is some explanation. In any case, a change of environment will do her the world of good.

FINGAL. As you say.

MADELEINE. Now, when I went to fetch her today I wanted to take the buggy but both our horses were lame, Mr Fingal.

FINGAL. I only just found out myself…

MADELEINE. Mike Wallace had to loan me his senile old mare. Only with great good fortune did I guess where Hannah had gone and luckily I found her before the cold and the rain had quite chilled her. You will see to the horses, Mr Fingal. How can such a thing have happened?

FINGAL. I don't know.

MADELEINE. Are the horses not your responsibility?

FINGAL. They are the boy's responsibility.

MADELEINE. Well, you will have to put him before his responsibilities.

FINGAL. Yes, madam.

MADELEINE. Our guests will no doubt want to ride abroad in the days they are here, so please see to it.

FINGAL. Yes, madam.

MADELEINE. This is not good enough.

FINGAL. I know.

MADELEINE *goes towards the door, but pauses near him before she leaves*.

MADELEINE. I want you to know that the gate lodge will continue to be at your disposal, for you and the boy, Mr Fingal, no matter what happens.

FINGAL. Thank you, madam.

MADELEINE. I believe Mrs Goulding has some warm stew. You will take some home for your supper.

FINGAL. Yes, madam.

MADELEINE *leaves.* FINGAL *stands there for a moment, then takes up his rifle and the horse blanket and exits. The lights change to a bright fresh morning. Birdsong is heard outside.* CLARE, *a young housemaid of about twenty or so, comes into the room carrying a tray with a silver teapot and cups and saucers which she places on the table. She is a local girl. She is quick-witted and understands the nuances of everything that goes on about her, but has the intelligence never to let on. The* REVEREND BERKELEY *follows her in, absent-mindedly reading a newspaper. He is about sixty and wears the black garb of a vicar. While he is jovial and likable for the most part, he is very serious when it comes to things he cares about. In these matters he brooks no contention and displays the confidence of a man who entirely believes in the uniqueness of his vocation. It is two days later, 10.20 a.m. Friday May 17th.*

BERKELEY. Thank you, Clare, for a delicious breakfast.

CLARE. You're welcome, sir.

BERKELEY. Oh, Clare, here…

CLARE *stands waiting awkwardly while* BERKELEY *roots in his waistcoat and trouser pockets for a coin he can't find.*

I'm sorry, Clare, I seem to have…

CLARE. No, sir.

BERKELEY. Will you remind me later to give you a coin?

CLARE. I'm sure I won't, sir!

She goes about her work setting the room up.

BERKELEY. Then I'll just have to remember myself. And I will!

CLARE. There is no need, sir, honestly.

BERKELEY. Little Clare Wallace! I scarcely believe the last time I saw you, you were this high. Do you remember me?

CLARE. Of course I do, sir.

BERKELEY. I have changed terribly, no doubt.

CLARE. No, sir.

BERKELEY. Whilst lying is always a sin, 'In certain lies there is but kindness.' Do you know who said that?

CLARE. No, sir.

BERKELEY. That's one of mine.

CLARE. Oh, very good, sir…

CHARLES AUDELLE *enters. He is in his mid-forties. He is striking-looking, somewhat intense, his eyes always searching for hidden depths.*

BERKELEY. Ah, Mr Audelle, you rise. And you have missed a delicious breakfast.

CLARE. Would you like me to bring you some up, sir?

AUDELLE. Please, don't go to any trouble. Is that tea?

CLARE. Yes, sir.

AUDELLE. Tea is fine.

BERKELEY. Slice of soda bread, Audelle?

CLARE. A slice of toast, sir?

AUDELLE (*without enthusiasm*). Em…

BERKELEY. Bring him some toast and some butter, Clare, should you be so kind.

CLARE. Yes, sir.

BERKELEY. Thank you, dear.

She exits.

(*Ominously.*) Well, sir, how did you sleep?

AUDELLE. Not well. And when I did drop away it was only to play host to some terrific nightmares.

BERKELEY. I thought as much.

AUDELLE. And you?

BERKELEY. I must confess, this place being something of a childhood home for me allied to the considerable relief to have arrived after such a turbulent journey, I had a passably comfortable night – but tell me, of what did you dream?

AUDELLE. I dreamt of a presence.

BERKELEY *pours some tea, watching* AUDELLE *take in the room.*

This is the room.

BERKELEY. This is the room. He hung the rope from a brace above the mirror, stepped off the mantelpiece and hung there until young Hannah had found him.

AUDELLE. The heart of the house. How old was she?

BERKELEY. Eight or nine. Yes. However, having heard the stories that have seeped under the door down the years, it is my belief that rather than stepping into oblivion he has found himself trapped here in an endless bad dream. Somehow caught between this world and the next. One of time's own prisoners.

AUDELLE. And Hannah has heard him…

BERKELEY. She has heard something.

AUDELLE. It is quite uncomfortable here, Berkeley.

BERKELEY. Is it bearable?

AUDELLE (*brusquely, advancing on the tea things*). Yes, it's bearable, but I suggest here is where we begin. When you begin.

BERKELEY. These occasions require a subtlety you might best leave to me, Charles.

AUDELLE. Oh, I intend to!

BERKELEY. For now, we are merely here to escort Hannah to Northamptonshire...

AUDELLE. Of course...

BERKELEY. However, when the household is more relaxed and we have gained a certain confidence, we may encourage such shadows that dwell here to make themselves manifest, which once apprehended... Ah!

He breaks off seeing that MRS GOULDING *has appeared in the doorway. Beside her is a little elderly lady known as* GRANDIE. *She has Alzheimer's disease; while she makes eye contact and smiles from time to time, she rarely speaks.*

MRS GOULDING. Reverend!

BERKELEY. Mrs Goulding! Why, you have not changed one bit! And Grandie!

BERKELEY *gives* MRS GOULDING *a kiss.*

MRS GOULDING. Oh, you say so...

BERKELEY. But it's true. It is true. You are radiant. And Grandie, how are you, my dear?

He offers her his hand.

MRS GOULDING. You remember the Reverend, Grandie. Will you shake hands?

GRANDIE *smiles vaguely, but does not shake hands.*

She'll be alright. Sometimes new people confuse her a bit. Sit down, Grandie, and we'll get you a slice of cake in a minute. That's right.

GRANDIE *does not sit, but places herself with her hand on the back of a chair, watching them.*

BERKELEY. Mrs Goulding, may I present my travelling companion, Mr Audelle?

MRS GOULDING (*shaking hands with* AUDELLE). You are welcome, sir. And anything we can do to make your stay more comfortable, you will tell us.

AUDELLE. I cannot see how that could be necessary.

BERKELEY. And this is Grandie, grandmother to the lady of the house. Quite a beauty in her day, Mrs Goulding.

MRS GOULDING. Oh, they all got their looks from her! Didn't they, Grandie? We'll get you a slice of cake now in a minute. You are looking hale and hearty, Reverend. And but I had no idea of the nature of your trip, sir! Is it true you will accompany Miss Hannah to England!

BERKELEY. For her wedding!

MRS GOULDING. Well, I am overcome. With joy, of course, but with sorrow too.

BERKELEY. Mrs Goulding has been almost a second mother to Hannah, Audelle.

MRS GOULDING. To both Hannah and her mother. I am like another grandmother to this house, I have been here so long.

BERKELEY. We used to call Mrs Goulding our 'maid mother'.

MRS GOULDING. Yes, yes!

BERKELEY. How often do I think of those everlasting summer days here at Mount Prospect, do you remember?

MRS GOULDING (*sadly*). Oh! At one time, Mr Audelle, meals of seven or eight courses would be served to a hundred guests or more here.

BERKELEY. At least!

MRS GOULDING. We had to heat gallons of hot water in a furnace by the kitchen door for servants to bring throughout the house every morning and evening, so as the hunters could soak their tired bones in brass hip baths we used to have in every room.

BERKELEY. Yes.

MRS GOULDING. This was all in Sir Arthur's time, of course, God rest him. Everything changed when he passed on, and that – God forgive me – amadán [*Irish for 'halfwit'*] Edward got his feet in under the table here. You know what he did, Reverend, don't you? Mr Audelle? You see that window there? He had it bricked up! So no one who called could see in, so he wouldn't have to entertain anyone who called and he could pretend there was no one home for weeks on end. Did you know that now?

BERKELEY. I did not know that.

MRS GOULDING. Yes. And little Hannah would be shoved away upstairs so as not to make noise, and not let on to the local children there was anyone here, I ask you! He alienated all their lovely neighbours. I shouldn't speak out of turn but – by Christ it vexes me to think how wonderful a place this was... before it all darkened in his time.

BERKELEY. Of course, but now... Well, this is a time for renewed celebration.

MRS GOULDING. Yes...

BERKELEY. And you are keeping well yourself, Mrs Goulding?

MRS GOULDING. I am middling well, thank God. What more can we ask? I'm sorry, your grace, and I'm sorry to you, sir. (*To* AUDELLE.) I didn't mean to speak ill of the dead. I don't know what overcame me.

AUDELLE. Please, do not be sorry on my account, Mrs Goulding, I assure you it is all most fascinating.

MRS GOULDING. It's just... to suddenly see yourself again after so long, Reverend. Suddenly all the time that seems to have just...

She wipes her eyes.

BERKELEY (*puts an arm round her*). No, no, come now, we are all happy. These feelings are as natural as a leaf falling to the earth. To know a little sadness on account of past joys is surely a cause for gratitude.

MRS GOULDING. You are right, sir.

MADELEINE enters, holding the door for CLARE, who carries a tray in with more tea, cups and some slices of toast under a napkin. MRS GOULDING supervises CLARE at the table, and they pour tea for all during the following.

BERKELEY. Madeleine!

MADELEINE. Berkeley.

BERKELEY. I have longed for this embrace.

He comes to her and embraces her. She allows him to kiss her cheek.

You cannot be eating well, Madeleine. Where have you gone? Ha ha ha! Oh, but you make me feel old. Finally I may introduce you. Lady Madeleine Lambroke, eternal succour to all in her protectorate; Mr Charles Audelle, gentleman of letters, philosophy and higher learning.

AUDELLE (*takes her hand*). Madam, such pleasure at last.

MADELEINE. We did not want to disturb you, Mr Audelle.

AUDELLE. With embarrassment, I must assure you I do not normally sleep on past seven o'clock, but we have not had comfort such as your wholesome dwelling provides for some nights now, and I am afraid I could not stir myself.

MADELEINE. I would have preferred to greet you last night, but the hour had grown so late, I had assumed you would not arrive until today.

BERKELEY. The bridge was half destroyed by so-called revolutionaries.

MRS GOULDING. Oh no!

BERKELEY. Yes! So we had to wait for the ferry, but the waters had risen so in the deluge, the pilot wouldn't go! We were loath to turn back and face our depressing lodgings at Jamestown so it was our good luck that a fisherman, who was determined to get home, took us across for two shillings. And thank you again, Clare, for admitting us so late. It was almost gone two o'clock!

MRS GOULDING. She is a well-mannered girl, is she not?

BERKELEY. Most decidedly!

MRS GOULDING. Say thank you, Clare.

CLARE. Thank you, sir.

MRS GOULDING. And Mr Audelle.

CLARE. Thank you, sir.

AUDELLE. No, thank you, Clare.

CLARE. Thank you, sir.

BERKELEY. Thank you, Clare.

MADELEINE. Yes... You will have noticed the deterioration of Jamestown, Berkeley.

BERKELEY. To an extent I had scarcely suspected, Madeleine. Our coach stopped near what we now realise was the workhouse.

MRS GOULDING. Oh, yes.

BERKELEY. Desperate men and women suddenly descended upon our coach. So numerous were the pale hands outstretched towards us, it was only later I understood that an insensible infant thrust before me by a cadaverous wild-eyed woman must surely have been deceased...

MADELEINE. Oh, Berkeley...

BERKELEY. Yes.

AUDELLE. I'm afraid it was so.

MRS GOULDING. Clare, why don't you run along and tell Miss Hannah there is tea in the drawing room.

CLARE. Yes, Mrs Goulding.

She goes.

MADELEINE. Times are hard here, Berkeley, there is no doubt. The meagre crop has failed again. But we have sought to assist those we can, have we not, Mrs Goulding?

MRS GOULDING. We have indeed, madam. Those as we can, God help us.

BERKELEY. Well, of course.

Pause.

MADELEINE. And you reside with the Reverend at present, Mr Audelle?

AUDELLE. I do, which is perhaps another reason I slept so late – I am not accustomed to the silent pleasures of a room of one's own. I am sorry to say the poor Reverend's snoring vibrates the slim walls of our modest apartment in Highgate at the best of times, but to share a room with him as I have these past few nights on our way down here, is to have one's very teeth shaken out of one's head!

They laugh.

BERKELEY. And I am blissfully unaware of it! More's the irritation! But we make good company, do we not?

AUDELLE. Oh, yes!

MRS GOULDING. Madam has always cried out in her sleep.

MADELEINE. Oh, not for a long time.

MRS GOULDING. And loud enough to wake me and I on the floor below.

BERKELEY. Oh dear! There is little so disturbing as the cry that reefs you to the surface!

MRS GOULDING. Now you said it!

MADELEINE. I haven't done that for a long, long time, Mrs Goulding.

MRS GOULDING. I wouldn't know – my hearing is not what it was.

Pause.

BERKELEY. You know, it occurs to me that each of us here in this room has been widowed.

MADELEINE. Oh, well, my sympathies, Mr Audelle.

AUDELLE. And mine to you, all.

MADELEINE. I have always envied Berkeley's faith in trying times. I must admit, I was never overly concerned for your welfare when Alice passed away – I knew your belief would hold strong. Certainly stronger than mine!

BERKELEY. My faith didn't protect me, Madeleine. It was my congregation who protected me. But only because Alice was beloved by all. Only when the Bishop took my lodgings away did I feel a loneliness that came and gutted me like a knife. That first winter I moved to London alone was... well, it was wretched.

MADELEINE. Your letters never betrayed that, Berkeley.

BERKELEY. Well. (*Short pause.*) But happily, on my travels – (*Touches* AUDELLE'S *shoulder.*) I met Mr Audelle, whose intellect and curiosity have given me great joy in our evenings together at home in Highgate. And in return he bears the burden of my company. Snoring and all!

CLARE *enters and holds the door open.* HANNAH *enters. She is seventeen and slender, alert with a keen perceptiveness of her situation and that of others. She wears spectacles and has a bandage on her right hand. She regards the room somewhat coolly.*

Can this be Hannah?

MADELEINE. This is Hannah.

BERKELEY. My word, the ten years that have passed since I was here had seemed but ten hours until now. Time itself has conjured a beautiful young lady where moments ago was a child. Do you recall me, cousin?

HANNAH. The last time I saw you we carved our names in the fairy tree near the gallops. Your initials are still there.

BERKELEY. That's right!

HANNAH. And you told me of a hanging you witnessed at Leitrim Gaol where the man called out to the Virgin Mary over and over after they put the sack on his head.

Short pause.

BERKELEY. Ha ha ha… And now we have come to take you away to be wedded to your love. Can it be so?

HANNAH. It certainly appears to be so.

BERKELEY. And I see, Madeleine, that my old sparring partner, the Bishop of Solsbury himself has been engaged to perform the ceremony. He may be a notoriously insufferable old bore, but one cannot fault him in matters of canon law. When you are married by him, it will be like an iron lock closing for ever in the eyes of God! (*Laughs.*) Permit me to introduce Mr Charles Audelle, Hannah, who has been so kind as to accompany me on my pleasant task. I trust you will find his company most instructive. Here… (*Produces a slim volume.*) is a copy of his book!

MRS GOULDING. His book!

HANNAH. Thank you.

HANNAH *takes it.* AUDELLE *offers her his hand. She presents him with her left, unbandaged, hand.*

AUDELLE. Pray, what has happened to your hand? Nothing serious, I hope.

HANNAH. I pierced it grabbing hold of some brambles the day before yesterday.

AUDELLE. I see.

BERKELEY. Mr Audelle is considered to be – especially by many young people, Hannah – one of the finest writers of the age in London. His mind is as delicate as any in his generation.

AUDELLE. Now please, Reverend.

HANNAH. I have heard of this book, sir. Weren't you recently accused of plagiarism?

AUDELLE. Well...

MADELEINE. Hannah...

BERKELEY. That was a misunderstanding...

MADELEINE. That's not a nice thing to say, Hannah.

AUDELLE. No, it's true, there was an... accusation...

HANNAH. I merely wanted to ask whom he was *accused* of plagiarising, Mother.

MRS GOULDING. What's plagiarise?

HANNAH. When you steal someone else's ideas and pass them off as your own.

MADELEINE. Hannah, that is not a kind thing to say.

AUDELLE. No, no, I'm afraid it has already been said, madam. Hannah is merely asking about something many already believe.

HANNAH. Who did you plagiarise?

MADELEINE. Hannah, you mean, who do they... say... he plagiarised...

HANNAH. Yes.

AUDELLE. Oh, some Germanic philosopher who was merely thinking along the same lines as myself. And while I allow he had already published some ideas similar to my own – they remained untranslated… and I was to all intents and purposes, unaware of them in their most recent form.

HANNAH. What was his name?

AUDELLE. Oh, I can barely pronounce it. Or bring myself to utter it.

HANNAH. You don't speak German?

AUDELLE. Certainly not well enough to dissect the latest in up-to-the-minute Prussian transcendental philosophy. No.

MADELEINE. Well, what a misfortune…

BERKELEY. The greater misfortune is that the bear pit of critical appraisal in London tends to be a hundred times more savage than the most animalistic assault in the wild.

MRS GOULDING. Dear God.

HANNAH. They had no case against you?

AUDELLE. Well, you see, some years ago I had the pleasure of visiting the universities of Tübingen and Jena. While my grasp of the language was rudimentary, like many, I was intoxicated by the potency of the lectures there. Certain ideas were… in the ether, like unplucked fruit upon an overripened vine, and while I had mistakenly assumed I was the first to give their utterance…

HANNAH. You were in fact not.

Pause.

AUDELLE. No.

BERKELEY. Such a thing can easily happen.

HANNAH. And you do not tire of philosophers inventing worlds where nobody lives?

MADELEINE. Oh, it is surely far too early in the day for such discussion, is it not? The sun is finally peeping out to beckon us to the garden.

BERKELEY. Precisely, Madeleine. Why don't we take our cups and...

HANNAH. What would you make of an opinion I read in a book, Mr Audelle, that male philosophers show particular eagerness in their desire to invent pictures of the world simply in order to argue about it? And they defend these pictures like an imaginary fort simply because boys never grow up.

They laugh.

MADELEINE. Hannah!

MRS GOULDING. Oh, boys never grow up!

AUDELLE. No, there is something in what Hannah says. I have seen the greatest thinkers of our age in the flesh, and I may tell you success does not so much change a person as reveal who they really are – and often it's ugly! But let me assure you that I, personally, have no need to invent a world to argue about — since the one I find myself in already confounds me quite enough.

BERKELEY. Well said, Audelle! And well said, Hannah! But now, as Madeleine says, the magic gardens call me here yet. We arrived in darkness and Mr Audelle has no idea of the beauty and wildness that surround us.

MADELEINE. There are plenty of old boots down by the kitchen door. You must spare your shoes after the rain. Mrs Goulding, will you show the gentlemen?

MRS GOULDING. Certainly, madam.

MADELEINE. Perhaps Grandie would like some air. Clare, you may leave the tea tray. Hannah and I will take a cup before we join you.

BERKELEY. Capital.

CLARE. Would you like some freshly brewed, madam?

MADELEINE. No thank you, I'm sure it's fine. We will join you presently.

AUDELLE. Thank you, Lady Lambroke. May I say what a pleasure it is to have finally met you both.

MADELEINE. You are welcome, sir.

MRS GOULDING *offers her arm to* GRANDIE, *who takes it.*

MRS GOULDING. Now, Grandie.

GRANDIE *suddenly goes and kisses* HANNAH *on the cheek.*

Now, there's a lovely kiss. Let's go and get some nice cake.

BERKELEY *leaves, followed by* AUDELLE, CLARE *and* MRS GOULDING, *who helps* GRANDIE *out. From the hall we hear* BERKELEY.

BERKELEY (*off*). Now, you see that painting above the fireplace?

AUDELLE (*off*). Oh yes, I saw that.

BERKELEY (*off*). That's the very view one is furnished with as we approach the gazebo.

MRS GOULDING (*off*). Come down this way, Mr Audelle.

AUDELLE (*off*). Yes, thank you, I'm coming.

MADELEINE. I see your temper has yet to abate.

HANNAH. Yes, well, I'm sorry, Mother. But to actually walk in and meet the men who are to take me away filled me with such anxiety I had spoken before I knew it.

MADELEINE. And must you articulate your anxiety with such bad manners? You know Lady Fitzmorris said a marriage

such as you have before you would be the envy of any
English girl, let alone an Irish girl who lives where the
prospect of a decent match is remote.

HANNAH. Really?

MADELEINE. Oh, so what would you prefer? One of the
Colonel's cockeyed twits, with not an idea in his head that
doesn't pertain to cards or fishing? Or wait until some
outcast is dispatched from a dissolute estate in the north? In
England you may reside three or four months of each year in
London. Can you imagine I had but a month there in my
whole life? I was presented to women and men of such
nobility my limbs were positively liquid in uncontrollable
acknowledgement of their position. And you will meet them
as an equal!

HANNAH. With a husband who bears me no love.

MADELEINE. Of course he will love you.

HANNAH. To say nothing of his alarming moral disarray.

MADELEINE. Youth is often a state of disarray, Hannah. As
Christians it behoves us to forgive an immature moment of
vagary, especially while he was under the spell of one who
should know better. I must say, I found his demeanour
almost penitential, and you yourself told me you thought his
mind was fine.

HANNAH. I said I had not found him as disagreeable as his
brothers, but only because he ignored me and left me alone.
It is his father who is attached to me. Surely you have seen
that.

MADELEINE. Oh, nonsense. He admires you.

HANNAH. All the time we were there the old man's eyes
followed me like black holes of insensible longing, while the
Marquis spoke to me only of dogs and guns. When he
deigned to actually ask me anything, my answers were
greeted with a decidedly unenthusiastic silence.

MADELEINE. So what, you will remain here at Mount
Prospect with its endless debts, enduring the hatred of those
who rent your holdings, until you too are finally turfed out?
You will be alone for ever – stigmatised as a bumpkin from
the colonies whose only dowry is the odour of our failure!

HANNAH. Yes, I know about dowries. You have bought your
way out of this place with whatever you could get for me!

MADELEINE (*grabbing* HANNAH's *arm*). How dare you!
How dare you?! You are not too old to be spanked, my girl.

HANNAH. Hit me then! If you must! Your marriage was
arranged for you and look how that ended!

MADELEINE *is lost for words for a moment, almost
shocked to tears.* HANNAH *pulls away.* MADELEINE
regards her.

MADELEINE. Yes, my marriage was arranged. What could I
know at nineteen years of age about husbands and how the
world works? The conscientiousness of our elders yielded an
excellent match which flourished into real love. What
happened to your father was due to… what he bore within
him, before we ever even met. As such, it was unavoidable
yet impossible to foresee. (*Pause.*) Hannah… please
understand how worried I have become. I undertake none of
this lightly. I know how you like the solitude of your room
and your books and your fire and your walks. But now you
will always have those things! And have them where you are
safe and well – within yourself. Where these sudden…
voices cannot distress you.

HANNAH. Yes, well, I wish I had never said anything about
that now.

MADELEINE. What would you have me do? Take Doctor
Henry's advice and put you in a hospital in Dublin?

HANNAH. What if they are trying to tell me something?

MADELEINE. Who?

HANNAH. The voices.

MADELEINE. Oh, Hannah! I cannot imagine they have anything good to say.

HANNAH. Perhaps they are warning me against the very plans you have made.

MADELEINE. Oh, come now.

HANNAH. Well, why not?

MADELEINE. Because the voices don't love you like I do. In time, you will see, when you have your own children, how you too would do anything for them. I will help you in your new life, with your new family.

HANNAH. You would come also?

MADELEINE. Well, of course.

HANNAH. No.

MADELEINE. What do you mean, no?

HANNAH. I forbid it, is what I mean.

MADELEINE. And go alone?

HANNAH. Why not? You have already arranged my chaperones.

MADELEINE. Hannah, I know you don't mean it.

HANNAH. No – I will endure Hell there with him or Hell here with you, but I will not endure both.

MADELEINE. Hannah!

HANNAH. If I am indeed to be mistress in my life, as you suggest, I will not be hampered by those who neither listen to, nor understand, my predicament. And if I must be sold, I will sell myself into personal sovereignty. And you, madam, may do as you wish.

MADELEINE. And leave me here?

HANNAH. But you have put me out!

BERKELEY *appears in the doorway holding a stick.*

BERKELEY. Ladies! The sky is burst through with sunlight behind the blackest clouds you have ever seen. Mr Audelle has described it as an aspect of the sublime! Please say you will join us as we walk down to the old pond.

MADELEINE. Of course.

BERKELEY. And I almost forgot to mention it! I have a letter from Hannah's prospective father-in-law.

MADELEINE. A letter?

BERKELEY *puts his stick down, takes an envelope from his inside pocket.*

BERKELEY. A letter he has asked me to read aloud before our assembled company after dinner one of these evenings. I must say I have rarely seen him so satisfied, Hannah. You will be a queen among his household.

MADELEINE. Let us walk then. Hannah. You will take my hand?

BERKELEY *examines the envelope as he goes out into the hallway.* HANNAH *regards* MADELEINE *for a moment, then steps forward and takes her hand.* MADELEINE *holds it tightly, grateful for the affection.* HANNAH *looks down.* MADELEINE *kisses* HANNAH's *hair. They regard each other in a moment of reconciliation, and leave.*

(*Off.*) You may lead the way, Berkeley.

BERKELEY (*off*). Yes, oh, just let me find my stick. The damp air gets me in my hip, I'm afraid.

BERKELEY *returns for his stick. He stands for a moment looking up at the brace above the mirror by the mantelpiece then follows them out. The lights change, bringing us to evening, two nights later, Sunday May 19th. It is about 9 p.m.*

There is still a trace of dusk in the sky. FINGAL *helps*
CLARE *light one or two oil lamps in the room.* FINGAL
then stands looking at a chessboard. CLARE *stands as*
though waiting for his attention, but leaves when AUDELLE
comes in, carrying a candle and a glass of red wine.

AUDELLE. Ah, Fingal… You see what I've done there.

FINGAL. You certainly know how to use those rooks.

AUDELLE (*seeing some decanters with liquor*). Brandy! Thank
God… (*Knocks back his wine and advances on the spirits.*)
Care for a drop?

FINGAL. Em… Maybe later.

AUDELLE. I don't think you can escape.

FINGAL. I think you may be right. (*Knocks over his king on*
the board.) You win, sir.

AUDELLE. A good game. Set them up again and you can be
white. Good God, did you see those poor wretches who came
into the yard for soup earlier on?

FINGAL (*setting up the pieces*). I did.

AUDELLE. I had no idea things were so bad.

FINGAL. Yes, they're bad from time to time.

AUDELLE. To my shame I had not the confidence to approach
them. Would they have spoken to me?

FINGAL. Ah, yes. They are a curious people; they would show
you great interest and courtesy, no doubt.

AUDELLE. I will greet them the next time.

FINGAL. Oh yes, they are always keen to learn English, sir.

AUDELLE (*savouring a large gulp of brandy*). Well, I have no
doubt, in the future, the Irishman will be beholden to no one
and walk amid the spirit of his age with pride.

FINGAL (*uncertainly*). Mm.

AUDELLE. No doubt. You were born near here, Mr Fingal?

FINGAL. I was.

AUDELLE. How do you all get on?

FINGAL. Who?

AUDELLE. You and the locals.

FINGAL. Ah, I'm neither one thing nor the other any more. Each side rejects you and everyone is suspicious.

AUDELLE. How unpleasant.

FINGAL. My father always said it suits the nature of a contrarian, Mr Audelle.

AUDELLE (*laughs*). Yes, it must rather. But this house is generous, is it not?

FINGAL. As generous as it may afford to be. Against the advice of many, her ladyship took in an orphan a few years ago. A boy who resides with me down at the gate lodge. He was given the name James Furay.

AUDELLE. Oh yes, I have seen him. I attempted to exchange greetings with him out on the steps this morning but he just looked at the earth.

FINGAL. He means no discourtesy. He's often silent in himself, but he's conscious of his great debt to the house in ways others I may mention are not. Here, sir.

FINGAL *holds out a coin to* AUDELLE.

AUDELLE. What's this?

FINGAL. Our wager, for the chess game.

AUDELLE. Oh no, sir, I will not accept your money.

FINGAL. A wager is a wager.

AUDELLE. No, no, come now.

FINGAL. I insist or we cannot play again.

AUDELLE. I was warned about you Irish. I'll tell you what, keep your money, but perhaps you might do me a small favour. (*Taking a piece of paper from his pocket*.) I have a doctor's script for some pain-relieving tincture which I was accustomed to buying in London. You see, I have a permanent jabbing in my lower back, sustained in a fall from a window some years ago. I had a small bottle with me, but unfortunately it cracked when we took our bags down from the coach in some haste in Jamestown the other evening. I asked the girl. Is her name Clare?

FINGAL. Yes.

AUDELLE. Yes, I asked her if she might take this and procure me some during her errands in town, but she returned it to me this morning saying Mrs Goulding forbade her to make the purchase! Can you believe that!

FINGAL. What's in it, sir?

AUDELLE. Nothing harmful!

FINGAL *takes the script, reading it…*

Medicinal herbs…

FINGAL. I see. Mrs Goulding has some firm ideas, I'm afraid.

AUDELLE. And you, sir?

FINGAL. Less so.

AUDELLE. You're a good man, Fingal.

FINGAL. I always pay my debts.

AUDELLE. Debts! Why, it's a little wager over a game of chess, not a bank loan, man. Only as long as it's no trouble.

FINGAL. It's no trouble, sir.

AUDELLE. I knew I could count on you. Goodness, this brandy evaporates so swiftly! Can I pour you one?

FINGAL. A… very small one only then, sir, to be social. Please allow me.

AUDELLE. Not at all. (*Pours them both quite large drinks.*) Have you eaten? We had some excellent trout earlier, at table with the curious young Hannah. Does she ever eat?

FINGAL. I assume she must.

AUDELLE. Our conversation ventured to an old tomb nearby which her mother seemed uneasy talking about. Do you know of it?

FINGAL. Up at Knocknashee?

AUDELLE. That's it.

FINGAL. It's just an old hole in the ground.

AUDELLE. What do they call it? The Queen's Tomb?

FINGAL. Some do. Others will not speak of it.

AUDELLE. What do you think it is?

FINGAL. I couldn't say. A doctor came over from Oxford when I was a boy. He said there's a passage underneath that's maybe been there for thousands of years.

AUDELLE. I'd love to see it.

FINGAL. Don't go up there on your own, sir.

AUDELLE. Is it frightening?

FINGAL. No, it's not frightening, but there are gangs of boys, and men, in that locality who would have certain perceived grievances with anyone they see wandering up from out of here. Up around the cottages at Knockmullen.

AUDELLE. I see.

FINGAL. If there's time I'll bring you up in the buggy maybe some morning, but please do not wander up there on your own, or at night.

AUDELLE. Understood.

FINGAL. The Reverend would know more about it than me.

AUDELLE. He knew much that he has forgotten.

FINGAL. He has indeed aged since I saw him.

AUDELLE. Well, that's what the Church of England has done.

FINGAL. Can I ask why he was he expelled, if that's not an impertinent question?

AUDELLE. Not at all. Perhaps you might ask him yourself if you have a spare hour or two to withstand his account.

FINGAL. You are not religious then, I take it.

AUDELLE. My religion is philosophy, sir. Do you pray?

FINGAL. No.

AUDELLE. Never?

FINGAL. Maybe in the night. I don't know.

AUDELLE. In the night.

FINGAL. Mmm.

Pause. FINGAL *looks down.* AUDELLE *regards him. The door opens and* HANNAH *enters. The men stand. She shuts the door.*

HANNAH. Am I disturbing you?

AUDELLE. Not at all. We were just talking about you. Please, sit by the fire. I was just sipping some brandy for my cold whereas Fingal is just drinking. I'm joking. Come. Join us.

HANNAH *comes into the room and stands looking into the fire, her hand on the back of a chair.*

FINGAL. I meant to tell you, miss; Liam O'Leary's mare had two beautiful foals. I thought you'd probably want to go and have a look before you leave.

HANNAH. Twins?

FINGAL. Yes.

HANNAH. Oh, I will.

Pause.

AUDELLE. How nice it is to sit here at your fire. Three nights ago we were at a ghastly inn at Jamestown. You must know it. We dined in the front parlour with a fire which, no matter how much coal the old pot boy shuffled on, never seemed to penetrate the damp chill of the room. The handful of diners as were present ate with their coats on. Nothing stirred in the street outside. The only sound was the hollow ticking of a clock in the hallway. Dear Lord. After a few restless, frozen hours in a narrow bed beside your kicking cousin, the Reverend, I went for a dawn walk that burnt my skin raw. Where the street ended and became countryside was the brick wall of the workhouse and a crowd of haggard-looking men and women turned to look at me with such alien ferocity I thought that should I ever find myself stranded here, I'd blow my brains out. Now, there's a thought.

FINGAL. So why come at all?

AUDELLE. Well, besides accompanying the Reverend... I came in search of ghosts, Mr Fingal.

FINGAL. Ghosts?

AUDELLE. Ghosts, Mr Fingal.

HANNAH. Why here?

AUDELLE. Well, Hannah, while the city of London will present the ghoulish at every corner, a true doorway to the eternal seems to demand the spiritual quietude and awesomeness as only desolate places such as Ireland may possess.

HANNAH. The vicar at Ballycliff says the eternal resides in the everyday things we see.

AUDELLE. Yet few ever seem to hear its song until it's too late!

HANNAH. Perhaps they are deaf.

AUDELLE. But you have heard, have you not? Here in this house?

HANNAH. Not just in the house, here in this very room, sir.

FINGAL. Miss Hannah…

HANNAH. Well, it's true, Fingal.

AUDELLE. Do tell us.

FINGAL (*warning her*). Miss Hannah…

HANNAH. When I was younger and I was learning the piano, often I would hear someone singing along with me somewhere in the house, a child. One day last year, I heard someone again. I had thought it was Clare, our maid, but when I went to check, there was no one outside. And then, only last Sunday while I sat writing, just here, where we are now, someone came in and shouted in my ear.

AUDELLE. What did they shout?

HANNAH. It was just a shout. It was a man's voice, right here in my ear.

FINGAL. It was the wind, or the door slamming on the hinges…

HANNAH. The day was as still as a stone, Mr Fingal, and I know what Mother has told you and asked you to play it down, but I know what happened and I won't be convinced of anything else.

AUDELLE. May I tell you what I think?

FINGAL. Mr Audelle, I think it would be better were we to take our dram and…

The door opens. MADELEINE *and* GRANDIE *come in with* CLARE, *who lights some candles.* MADELEINE *looks on the company disapprovingly.* FINGAL *and* AUDELLE *rise to their feet guiltily.* BERKELEY *comes in behind her waving a letter.*

BERKELEY. Gather ye! Gather ye! I bring news from beyond the realm.

HANNAH. Oh, Berkeley, please, must you read it?

BERKELEY. Of course I must! I am under strict instructions. It will be read 'before the host who inhabit the child's home,' to quote Lord Ashby directly.

HANNAH. This is outrageous.

MADELEINE. Hannah, we will all watch our manners.

BERKELEY. He assures me it is not long and I have no doubt it is perfectly innocuous. Now, where are my spectacles?

HANNAH. Oh God...

MRS GOULDING *puts her head round the door. She wears her best evening dress. It may be quite old but has a striking amount of gold brocade and ornamentation.*

MRS GOULDING. Have I missed the letter?

MADELEINE. No, you are just in time.

HANNAH. Of course! Come in! Come in! Clare, do take a seat.

MRS GOULDING (*lampooning* HANNAH's *concerns. She is drunk and consequently emotional and energised*). Oh, the drama of it all! You would swear it was your funeral you were heading off to rather than a wedding that would be the envy of any young girl in the world. Will Grandie take a sherry? She will, won't you, Grandie?

BERKELEY. Is that Irish whiskey I spy?

MRS GOULDING. It is. Only freshly bought – and sampled, personally – this morning.

BERKELEY. My throat is… (*Waves his hand in front of his throat.*)

MRS GOULDING. Clare, pour a drop for the Reverend. I will have a drop also, begging your ladyship's grace. Clare, you may have a small sherry, and one for Grandie.

CLARE. Madam?

MADELEINE. Not for me, Clare, pour yourself a sherry.

MRS GOULDING. A small sherry. But pour me a fitting measure of our Lord's tears.

AUDELLE. And I will join you if I may. Fingal?

FINGAL *hands* AUDELLE *his glass.*

REVEREND. Easy, my friend. Mr Audelle has been sipping spirits for that terrible cold he has had this past year and a half.

There is some laughter at this.

MRS GOULDING. Well, as Mr O'Connell said in his speech at Loughferry – 'It will take a strong draught to blow back the veil of confusion!'

Laughter.

AUDELLE. Well said.

BERKELEY. Now, if we are settled… (*Unfolds the letter.*) He has such a fine hand. (*Sniffs the paper.*) And always the best Corinthian ink.

MRS GOULDING. But of course. Clare, settle!

CLARE *looks for a seat.*

FINGAL (*offering* CLARE *a seat*). Clare, please.

MRS GOULDING. Leave her where she is. She is at work.

FINGAL. As are we, Mrs Goulding. Clare, take a seat here.

MADELEINE. Yes, sit here, Clare.

CLARE *goes to* FINGAL's *seat.*

HANNAH. This is agony.

AUDELLE. There is seldom sport without it.

MRS GOULDING. Just sit somewhere, child, you will spill your drink. Do you think you could have fit any more in that glass? Look at it!

MADELEINE. Hannah! Berkeley, please begin.

BERKELEY. Ahem... 'My dear Miss Hannah, Tonight the wind rages about the eaves and far across our lands the animals huddle for warmth. The house creaks about me, and yet as I sit here long after all have retired and the last embers colden...' Is that a word? (*Squints at it.*) Colden?

MADELEINE. I don't think so.

HANNAH. Oh God...

MRS GOULDING. The word is 'encolden'.

BERKELEY. Is it?

FINGAL. I have never heard that word.

MRS GOULDING. To encolden – to grow cold, or lose warmth.

MADELEINE. You are having us all on now, Mrs Goulding.

MRS GOULDING. Doesn't his lordship use it himself in his letter?

AUDELLE. Perhaps he has partaken of the early dew. (*Helping himself to a drink.*) Fingal?

FINGAL. No, thank you.

BERKELEY. Audelle, may I continue?

AUDELLE. Forgive me. A smallish dram as I have grown just a tad encoldened.

Laughter.

MRS GOULDING. I am also a tad encoldened. (*Brings* AUDELLE *her glass*.)

BERKELEY. Alright, settle down. 'The house creaks about me, and yet as I sit here long after all have retired and the last embers colden, somehow the memory of your visit to our house last Easter is alive in the mind, as though I am staring through the glass wall of time and observing those happy days when you and your beautiful mother dwelt amongst us and lit our house like a tiny sun. I hear you playing the piano. It still echoes through our hallways; a joyous yet saddening music which only reminds us of your absence and your longed-for presence.

That my eldest, and may I say most time-consuming, son should have you as his prospective bride brings a secret joy to my heart and I sing its mysterious melody tonight. I do admit I may have burdened him with the unrealistic expectations of an inexperienced father – burdens I have perhaps never placed on my subsequent sons – and thus he may have struggled in the past to accept his place in the world satisfactorily. But I am filled with confidence now, because I know your companionship will be, for him, both the steady ballast of his moral bearing and a guiding hand on his tiller.' (*Clears his throat*.) Ahem.

'Until you are with us I send you thanks and warm wishes in recognition of the gifts you have already granted us; your grace and your temperate solemnity. I hear the birds calling far away in the forest and I know that dawn is approaching. I will pass this letter to my rock and spiritual advisor, Reverend Berkeley, and should all befall as one may dare to hope, he stands before you reading it now while I languish hundreds of miles away on my own fair isle of England, but my words are now among you and blessed to be so. My friends, I remain yours, George, 16th Earl of Loughborough and Northampton, humble servant of the King and our Lord God Almighty.'

He lowers the letter.

MRS GOULDING. Well, now, that's what I call a letter!

BERKELEY. I am not in the least surprised. His lordship is a thoughtful creature. He has worried so about his boys since the departure of their dear mother, and he longs to see them settled. He is an especially intuitive soul and I believe he has spotted in Hannah a unique aspect I myself have often wondered about.

GRANDIE. The dog is at the door.

MRS GOULDING. Shush now, Grandie, and drink your sherry.

BERKELEY. Those of a spiritual bent can see that someone of Hannah's beauty must be in touch with something *elemental*. In my numerous and varied travels on the British Isles, I have encountered a great many people in a great many places and please hear me without prejudice when I say that certain persons have a strange energetic effect on the very nature of time itself. His lordship has apprehended this. Hear the passion with which he addresses Hannah as though she is still in his house, one can almost sense his terror he will not be close to her unique atunement again.

MADELEINE. Berkeley, you will frighten the girl…

BERKELEY. Oh, come. (*With sudden unexpected seriousness.*) We all know that Hannah hears echoes of a past none else can hear.

MADELEINE (*straining to be jovial*). I must forbid this conversation. Such seriousness! That letter has quite unsettled me. Clare, tidy up.

MRS GOULDING. Madam, the Reverend is correct. Do not be unsettled by that letter and under no circumstances reconsider your plans. The girl must go to England. Look at the creatures who inhabit this place around us. If she stays here, what will she inherit? The ingratitude of the wretches who skulk about this island? Who are these people? The wildness in them. And the badness in them. They are only

filthy tinkers the half of them. I grew up in Jamestown,
Reverend. My people had a decent shop. We were schooled
until we were eleven years of age. The women out here
would thieve anything. And when we serve them soup all out
in the back there. All in the yard, the tables lined up, eight
gallons of water, onions, turnips, the four legs of a lamb,
mind you…

FINGAL. Now, Mrs Goulding, you are too exercised…

MRS GOULDING. Bags of rice in the stew, bags of meal. All
out there this year and in 1821 as well. The thieving red-
haired look they'd give you, as they hunch over carrying it
all out in under the trees out there so as not to share it with
each other. The suspicion! They are in league with the devil
the half of them. Clare, replenish me.

She holds her glass out to CLARE, *who takes it to get her a
drink of whiskey.*

MADELEINE. You can scarcely believe such a thing, Mrs
Goulding.

MRS GOULDING. I don't have to believe it, madam! It's just
true! Take Mistress Hannah to England, and if you must go
yourself, then go. Grandie will be happy with me here. There
is less magic in England, and more good sense. The glow
that comes off Hannah will bring her good luck there. Here it
will only darken all her evenings. The fairies are jealous of
her.

FINGAL. Mrs Goulding… For Jaysus' sake!

MRS GOULDING. Do not dare presume to lecture me, sir! You
are lost in your own squalor. Sure wasn't my own son nearly
taken from us by a fairy woman?

MADELEINE. Mrs Goulding…

MRS GOULDING. He was only sixteen and came back down
from working on the boats out at McKenna Island,
Reverend. On Christmas Eve he was dressing up in a new

shirt and collar. I hardly saw him he was gone so much over the holiday – to meet with a woman he'd met on the road, no less, standing in a hedge! I knew it was no good. Night after night he left to meet her, hurling abuse at me when I tried to stop him. The colour in his face was like the ashes in the fire. He was sick in his heart. He near faded away before my eyes over the days. Till I got the priest to come and bless him while he lay asleep one morning, stretched out in front of the hearth. When he came to he cried his eyes out. He saw that I had saved him. And I had. Yes.

Pause.

MADELEINE. Yes, well…

AUDELLE. I believe you, Mrs Goulding. Your son was lucky to have you to dispel this sapping spirit. I myself had no such good luck until I met our esteemed Reverend. Once, in Spitalfields, I went into a tent to see an exhibit – a monster so they claimed. Of course, the pitiful creature was no more than a misshapen dwarf who was clearly a halfwit. But I saw a monster there all the same. It lurked behind the pain in his eyes. Such a look will always haunt me. And for tuppence I was implicit in heaping further grief upon his soul. The glance he darted at me held such a longing for release and understanding while his keeper barked and hit him. Yes, a monster surely followed among the dirty hoard I kept company with that night as we crawled up the dock wall looking for any dim lantern in a laneway. An elemental darkness is already inside each of us, how we explain it to ourselves is for each of us to bear. Anyone with a gift such as Hannah's is like a beacon in the dark.

BERKELEY. That's right.

MADELEINE. Oh, give me a drink, someone.

MRS GOULDING. Clare…

CLARE *gets a drink for* MADELEINE.

HANNAH. Mother…?

MADELEINE. A small sherry.

MRS GOULDING. A small sherry for Miss Hannah, Clare.

CLARE. Yes, ma'am.

GRANDIE. The old man wipes his feet and says, 'We're home from the fields!'

MRS GOULDING. And for Grandie. Yes, Grandie.

HANNAH. Mama saw a ghost when she was a girl.

MADELEINE. Hannah…

HANNAH. You did.

MADELEINE. I didn't. I have never seen a ghost.

HANNAH. You told us you saw one when you were sixteen in a hotel in London.

MADELEINE. It wasn't in a hotel and I told you it was just a dream.

BERKELEY. Where was it, Madeleine?

MADELEINE. This is ridiculous. I didn't see a ghost, Berkeley. I had a nightmare while I was staying at Great-Uncle Cyril's house in Holborn.

AUDELLE. Oh, do tell us.

MADELEINE. There is nothing to tell. I had eaten too many Belgian sausages before retiring. And not being used to it, I'd had two or even three glasses of white wine. When I went to bed, it being a strange house, I had trouble sleeping. I woke up, wrapped in a knot of blankets and I… I… dreamt I saw a young man standing just inside the door.

AUDELLE. Oh my word.

BERKELEY. They all have the gift.

MADELEINE. It was a dream, Berkeley. And Hannah knows she is making mischief to bring it up.

AUDELLE. Did he say anything?

MADELEINE. Who?

AUDELLE. The young man in your bedroom.

MADELEINE. Oh, I, you know how it is, for a moment I presumed he was real and I said, 'What do you want?' And he told me that…

HANNAH. That he had been murdered…

MADELEINE. Thank you, Hannah. He said he had been murdered in this room many years before. He raised his arm and pointed across the floor. I followed his gaze and… there was his body, lying on the mat under the window, as though it had been severely beaten. With that I let out a scream which brought my aunt and cousin running to my aid. You may imagine my embarrassment as I tried to explain I had merely been experiencing a heavy bout of indigestion.

BERKELEY. Or a visit from the beyond…

MADELEINE. I don't think so, Berkeley. A child will dream.

BEREKELY (*agreeing with her as though she has made his point for him*). Yes.

AUDELLE. Can you tell me, Mrs Goulding, or Mr Fingal, the other evening as we lodged in Jamestown I heard it mentioned that a child was once taken by the fairies out near, was it Drumshanbo?

MRS GOULDING (*snorts*). Once!?

BERKELEY. Yes, I had heard many such stories on my visits here as a boy but none yet so specific as this one.

MADELEINE. Oh, must we?

FINGAL. It's not true. None of that is true.

AUDELLE. Mrs Goulding?

MADELEINE. No more of this. Mrs Goulding, you put your
glass away and prepare Grandie for her bed. Clare, you will
start tidying up. Thank you very much.

MRS GOULDING. I admit the whiskey has dulled me, sir.

AUDELLE. We burn but for a brief moment!

HANNAH. No, it's true. A man in Drumshanbo lost his
daughter.

MADELEINE. Hannah, go to bed.

HANNAH. They took his little girl. No one denies it. His name
was Fogarty or Fergus. I forget.

MADELEINE. Have you not heard me?

BERKELEY. Madeleine… we are just talking and enjoying
ourselves, let her tell us the story. You were always too quick
to stamp your foot. Clare, sit down. Don't be a fuddle
duddle, Madeleine. Tell us, Hannah.

HANNAH. Her father had drunk himself so completely
senseless he fell asleep under the bushes out by a country
road. They say he met someone in there while he was asleep
and they took him before the Fairy King that night and he
begged them for a drink.

MADELEINE. He was dreaming!

HANNAH. There was uproar in the court of the Fairy King at
this mortal man's impudence, and the King of the Fairies
asked what would he give in return for his fill of drink? 'I
would give you anything, had I anything to give,' said
Fogarty. 'Would you give me your finest jewel?' asked the
King. 'Had I a jewel to give you, it would be yours,' said
Fogarty. At this the court all burst out laughing. Music
started playing and Fogarty did a drunken jig before them
all, falling about the place until he collapsed and awoke at
the bottom of the hill and beside him were three full bottles

of poitín. So of course, no one saw him for a week then. He went up the coast and was brought home senseless in the back of a hay cart from Queensfort.

MADELEINE. Hannah, where do you hear this nonsense? I am ashamed!

HANNAH. And when he got back to where he lived with his daughter, she wasn't there. He searched for her. He assumed his neighbours were taking care of her, but none of them had seen her for days. Forlornly he sat in his cottage until at night he heard a snuffled weeping and went to his child's cot, where a shape stirred beneath the blanket. He praised God and reached down to the child, but was horrified to find instead a wizened little creature all purple and black and grey-haired, like a tiny little old woman gaping up at him. He ran, wailing, from his house, knowing he had given the fairies his finest jewel – for what? For nothing.

MADELEINE. Has our conversation really degenerated to this extent? Stories of squalid, alcohol-drenched dreamers who pass out... and meet the... the little people...

HANNAH. I never said they were little.

BERKELEY. There has always been something here. I have always felt it.

MADELEINE. That's just your memories and a decidedly childhood association with this place, Berkeley. You are a romantic.

BERKELEY. But Hannah has heard it. (*Short pause.*) I believe people get trapped here, Madeleine. Even those we love...

Pause.

MRS GOULDING. Clare, you are excused.

BERKELEY. Let her stay.

MRS GOULDING. She's terrified, look at her.

FINGAL. Are you?

CLARE *shakes her head.*

AUDELLE. She's more terrified of walking all the way down to the scullery on her own in the dark.

FINGAL. Let her be, Mrs Goulding.

BERKELEY. There is something here, Madeleine, Hannah has heard it.

Pause.

MADELEINE. No.

BERKELEY (*to* HANNAH). Have you not?

MRS GOULDING. Holy Mary, Mother of God, pray for us sinners, now and at the hour of death, amen.

BERKELEY. There is no cause for alarm. I have prayed for souls who were trapped in Nottingham, Gateshead...

AUDELLE. Edinburgh.

BERKELEY. Edinburgh.

MADELEINE. Berkeley, I forbid this.

BERKELEY. While the light of so many living souls are gathered together here, we should not lose our opportunity to pray. Will you not pray with us, Madeleine? A prayer before bed, nothing more. I assure you...

MADELEINE. Hannah is a young girl, Berkeley.

BERKELEY. She is a woman who is to be married.

MADELEINE. She was always a dreamer.

MRS GOULDING. Do not stick a blade in the hornet's nest, Reverend.

MADELEINE. Hannah has always loved stories. Her head is always in a book. She didn't hear anything.

HANNAH. But I did.

MADELEINE. Berkeley...

HANNAH. I did hear it. Someone shouted at me here in this room. They screamed right in my ear and if there's no one who believes me I still don't care.

BERKELEY. Shh... shhh... my child...

FINGAL. You are scaring the women, sir.

BERKELEY. No, no. There is no reason for fear. We are modern people now. And as such, we know that the spirit realm resides outside of time. As human animals with material bodies we are unfortunately trapped always in this moment and we don't know how to escape it. We cannot measure the past because it is gone. We cannot measure the future because it has yet to occur and we cannot measure the present because it slips away the instant we try to grasp it. Yet a spirit, a spirit exists in God's time where all moments are one eternal moment and all time is now. Yet man is, consider ye, both spirit and matter. Our spirit longs to commune with the eternal yet is all the while trapped within the prison of time itself, longing to be free. Those who have seen a ghost will say it is shadowy and transparent, often only glimpsed on the edge of sleep – why? Because we have not seen it with our physical eye, rather it is an imprint upon the imagination where our spirit apprehends the infinite. A spirit has spoken with Hannah. No more, no less. (*Gives a little laugh.*) There is nothing to fear! Now, before we retire for the evening, let us pray...

MADELEINE. Berkeley.

BERKELEY. No, no, just a bedtime prayer before we retire. That's all. (*Joins his hands and closes his eyes.*) Dear Lord, we beseech thee, deliver the lost and restless wanderer from the nightmare of darkness that engulfs us. Tell us, traveller, what do you want here? What is the nature of your plight? Tell us, in the name of Almighty God, what time are you lost in? (*Pause.*) Who is here? (*Pause.*) Who is here?

Pause.

MADELEINE. Berkeley...

BERKELEY. Who is here? (*Louder.*) WHO IS HERE? (*Louder again.*) WHO IS HERE??!

Pause. There is a sudden deafening bang like a gunshot over their heads. It seems to blow the room apart with its sonic impact. Their drinks go flying, cups are dropped. Each instinctively cries out and cowers...

MRS GOULDING. Dear God, dear God...

FINGAL (*getting up and looking around the room*). What was that? (*Opens the door to look out into the hallway.*)

MADELEINE (*to* BERKELEY). What did you do? (*Pause.*) What did you do?

BERKELEY. I... I don't know... I...

MADELEINE. How dare you? I asked you! In my house!

FINGAL *wanders back in.*

AUDELLE. There is a spirit here.

MADELEINE. You will be quiet, sir! You are a guest here, Mr Audelle, and I will kindly ask you to mind your manners. Berkeley, you will have nothing more to drink. Mrs Goulding, take Clare down and put the kettle on. Hannah, you will retire.

HANNAH. Mama, I...

MADEINE. You will retire!

HANNAH. Yes, Mama.

MRS GOULDING. Come, Clare... Help me with Grandie.

GRANDIE *pulls away from* MRS GOULDING.

MADELEINE. Leave her be, Mrs Goulding. Go and warm some water.

MRS GOULDING. Yes, madam.

MRS GOULDING *signals furiously to* CLARE *to help her and they start tidying up.*

BERKELEY. Madeleine. I am only trying to help.

MADELEINE. Well, you are lost in the clouds, Berkeley, you always were. We will discuss this in the morning.

There is a loud knocking at the front door. They all fall silent.

MRS GOULDING. Oh my Lord…

FINGAL *goes.*

MADELEINE. It is probably James Furay come to see what commotion we have made. What kind of example can we be setting for the boy?

AUDELLE. But what was it? What was that report?

MADELEINE. Well, it was… it was…

Silence. FINGAL *steps into the room.*

FINGAL. Madam, there is a constable outside.

MADELEINE. A constable?

FINGAL. Yes there has been a…

MADELEINE. Yes? (*Pause.*) What is it, Mr Fingal?

FINGAL. A terrace of houses in Jamestown that belong to this estate has collapsed.

MRS GOULDING. Oh, madam.

FINGAL. A number of families were trapped inside…

MADELEINE. I see.

MRS GOULDING. Oh no…

FINGAL. The constable has ridden out to inform you.

Pause.

MADELEINE. Yes, well, bring him in and see if he wants some soup. Mrs Goulding.

MRS GOULDING. Take him downstairs, Clare.

CLARE. Yes, madam.

CLARE *goes. Pause.*

MADELEINE. Where is he?

FINGAL. He is in the parlour.

MADELEINE *looks at* BERKELEY.

BERKELEY. Come, we will go to him.

BERKELEY *and* MADELEINE *leave. The others stand or sit in a state of numb distress.*

MRS GOULDING. What have we done?

The light changes to afternoon. Sunlight falls in through the foliage outside. It is two days later, Tuesday May 21st, around 3 p.m. HANNAH *sits near the window, writing.* GRANDIE *sits near the fireplace on a stool.* AUDELLE *comes in.*

AUDELLE. Where is everybody?

HANNAH. They are gone to Jamestown with Colonel Bennett to see the ruins of the terrace.

AUDELLE. Oh.

HANNAH. Were you asleep?

AUDELLE. I must have been. Is that tea?

HANNAH. Yes, Clare just brought it. For the first time I am glad that the Reverend was here.

AUDELLE *gets himself some tea.*

AUDELLE. I am gratified to hear that.

HANNAH. Everyone hates us, Mr Audelle.

AUDELLE *takes some tea.*

Mr Audelle.

Pause.

AUDELLE. Yes.

HANNAH. What happened in here the night before last.

AUDELLE. Yes.

HANNAH. Do you think it had something to do with what has happened in Jamestown?

AUDELLE. Absolutely.

HANNAH. Does it not bother you?

AUDELLE. Why would it bother me?

HANNAH. Because people have died, Mr Audelle, children have died, in property we owned and we heard something like a thunderclap here while we were... we were... Well... whatever we were doing, I haven't slept since. Are you only outwardly calm, or are you truly calm because you have no investment in this place and couldn't care less who lives or dies?

AUDELLE. Quite the reverse.

HANNAH. Your hands are remarkably steady then, sir. I can barely raise a cup.

AUDELLE. I administered ten drops of laudanum to myself at noon.

HANNAH. Does it work?

AUDELLE. Oh yes, it works – and I might say the local brew is thankfully intense. You see, I have always been susceptible to a kind of spiritual... distress, in certain places. Though I have never actually apprehended a spirit. Unlike you.

Short pause.

HANNAH *thinks about this and returns to her letter.*

HANNAH. You will excuse me, I hope, I am trying to finish a letter I promised to send by today.

AUDELLE *drinks some tea and looks at* GRANDIE.

GRANDIE. And may I ask you, sir; I don't know did you ever see a king around these parts that has mirrors where his eyes should be?

AUDELLE. A... king?

GRANDIE. Yes, he seems to be a kind of a king, with regal bearing, you understand, but he has mirrors instead of eyes. You see yourself when he looks at you! He's out under the trees there sometimes. Did you know about St Patrick?

AUDELLE. St Patrick?

GRANDIE. Yes, St Patrick.

AUDELLE. I... think I know about him.

GRANDIE. Well, he told me who St Patrick really was. St Patrick was a gold prospector! Did you know that? I didn't. They found gold all up in the hills around Cavan and Monaghan. St Patrick came with the good book all about Jesus Christ. That's how they always come, you see, and he said to everyone, 'These gods you have are no good,' apparently. He said he'd tell them all about this better God he knew all about – a very meek God you see, and while they were all busy praying to this terribly meek God, called Jesus Christ who was dreadfully meek, St Patrick took all the gold away! Yes, he told me all about St Patrick.

AUDELLE. I see. Well, thank you for telling me that.

GRANDIE. Yes.

Pause.

AUDELLE (*turning away from* GRANDIE). Do you have any friends who live nearby, Hannah?

HANNAH. When we were younger I used to play with James Furay, a boy my mother took in. But he lives down in the gate lodge with Mr Fingal now. I sense he has been encouraged not to speak with me.

AUDELLE. I am sorry.

HANNAH (*writing*). I had another friend, Elizabeth Argyle who lived at Drumsna. We used to share a tutor here but she got married last year and now lives in County Cavan.

AUDELLE. Is she happy?

HANNAH. She has a baby who has made her happy.

AUDELLE. You will be loved when you are married, Hannah.

HANNAH (*finishes her letter, lifting the paper to dry the ink*). We do not all pine for the love of a protector, Mr Audelle. Lord Ashby's estate is vast. We will have our own house. Clean linen at breakfast, as much hot water as a person may want. I am to receive an allowance and have a carriage at my personal disposal along with weekly French lessons.

AUDELLE. I'm sure your material circumstances will improve, Miss Lambroke, indeed I believe you will rule your domain just as you do here.

HANNAH. You think so?

AUDELLE. I know so. But I do not believe you expect such things will make you happy.

HANNAH. You are very frank, Mr Audelle.

AUDELLE *shrugs and goes to pour himself some tea.* HANNAH *watches him.*

Do you know anything of my fiancé?

AUDELLE. I know. That he made the Duke of Wellborough's widow pregnant and that both she and the child perished before she could bring it forth, thus freeing him conveniently of his obligations? (*Beat.*) Thus freeing him to marry?

HANNAH. He was under her spell.

AUDELLE. Well, of course he was. And now he isn't.

Pause.

HANNAH. You know, Elizabeth Argyle heard a great deal about you when we learned you were lodging with my cousin.

AUDELLE. Really?

HANNAH. Yes. And none of it encouraging. (*Pause*.) Is it true you abandoned your wife?

AUDELLE. It is.

HANNAH. And your child?

Pause.

AUDELLE. When I met my wife I was not much older than you.

HANNAH. What's that supposed to mean?

AUDELLE. Just that you... You might think me naive, but when I looked into her face – her grey eyes were so disarming I had always felt as though I was looking *through* her eyes into something so meaningful that I swore that somehow I could behold God there. And thus every moment was a moment of adoration.

HANNAH. How nice for her.

AUDELLE. Her father had lent us a remote cottage while I tried to write. The weather had been particularly bad. We hid inside from the continuous deluge. The child was sick and crying. My wife was sick. And then I was sick. Very sick. And one morning I looked into my wife's face at breakfast and I realised I could no longer see into the eternal. It was as though a shutter had come down and God had absented himself. And I... accepted that and I tried to... I tried to... but then, while attending Sunday service one morning in March, I thought I spied God again, peering at me from the eyes of another – two others – sisters.

HANNAH. I had scarcely believed it could be true.

AUDELLE. Yes, emboldened by fortifying my brandy with laudanum, I embarked on what I can only describe as sordid interior escapades at their cottage for days on end.

HANNAH. Is it true you turned your wife away with your dead child in her arms?

AUDELLE. No, that's not true. She had walked several miles in the rain with the child to find me one night and… (*Short pause*.) But you must understand how insensible I was. I thought I had heard her voice below the window while I lay deep beneath the blankets. But I… I was… The facts are that the child passed some days afterward – not that night. (*Short pause*.) I endeavoured to take my own life some several times afterwards and I ended up living in London's parks. If not for your cousin, the Reverend – I would have probably died in the madhouse.

HANNAH. Perhaps I can never understand your actions concerning your family, Mr Audelle, and I know they are unforgivable, but I do know what it is to feel alone. The sheer effort it takes for me to appear normal has become so painful, sometimes I just want to put my head down and cry. Because I know now there is something real, separate from me – (*Short pause*.) and I know it's waiting for me, calling for me to do what my father did. It knows how tired I am. It knows how old being so exhausted and lonely can make you feel.

She is unable to contain her feelings. She wipes her eyes.

AUDELLE. You shouldn't feel old, Hannah.

HANNAH. I know, but when there's nothing to look forward to because you are so tired you just want to sleep all day long, but then you don't want to sleep for fear of what you might see or hear because you know that Hell itself is that moment where something happens to you that you know you can never explain, a moment that makes your vision tremble and you simply cannot continue because that moment never ends, and you know in your heart that belief cannot save you and you suspect that even death cannot save you, because when you are in Hell you know only one thing – that only nothingness is holy. (*Pause. Composes herself*.) Will you give me some laudanum?

Pause.

AUDELLE. If you like.

HANNAH. Where is it?

AUDELLE. In my pocket.

HANNAH. How do you take it?

AUDELLE. It is best poured in a little drop of brandy.

HANNAH. Will you pour me some?

> AUDELLE *goes to the drinks and pours her a brandy. He hands her the glass, then takes a small bottle from his inside jacket pocket. She holds out her glass.*

AUDELLE. The old stones up at the top of the hill…

HANNAH. The Queen's Tomb?

AUDELLE. Yes. Will you take me up there for a look?

HANNAH. What for?

AUDELLE. To just behold their magic.

> HANNAH *shrugs.*

HANNAH. If you like.

AUDELLE. Thank you.

> *He takes the top from the bottle of laudanum and goes to pour some into* HANNAH's *glass.*
>
> *The lights fade.*
>
> *End of Act One.*

ACT TWO

*Night, around midnight on Thursday May 23rd. GRANDIE is
sitting quietly near the fireplace as the fire dies. A wind is
picking up outside. HANNAH slowly plays a single note over
and over on the piano. There is a knock. The door to the
hallway opens and BERKELEY and AUDELLE enter. They
stand near the door, wrapped up in their coats.*

BERKELEY. Ah, some nighthawks! We didn't expect anyone to
still be up.

HANNAH (*rises*). Sometimes Grandie gets up. She never
knows when it's night-time.

BERKELEY. Well, we had a lovely moonlight stroll. To walk
off our dinner. Are we alone?

HANNAH. Everyone was in bed.

BERKELEY. Of course. Will we join you for a moment?

BERKELEY *and* AUDELLE *come further into the room.*

HANNAH. What time is it?

BERKELEY. It's after midnight! Goodnight, Grandie. How
fares the world? You know, I was only saying to Mr Audelle,
Thursday was always my favourite day of the week when I
was a little boy. It was the one day I was permitted out of the
nursery and could sit all afternoon with my mother while my
father wrote his lectures. I keenly remember the fascination
and privilege I felt in their company. Every Thursday.

AUDELLE. I used to watch my father writing his sermons.

BERKELEY. I saw him preach. He was a great believer in the
corrective terror of hell and damnation which lent his oratory
an extra impassioned forcefulness, I remember! (*Laughs.
Pause.*) You look tired, Hannah.

GRANDIE *looks at him blankly then gives a slight smile of acknowledgement, turning her face back to the fire.*

HANNAH. Well, yes I am, rather.

BERKELEY. Mr Audelle tells me you were kind enough to bring him up to the Queen's Tomb yesterday.

HANNAH. Yes.

BERKELEY. But you didn't stay long.

Short pause.

HANNAH. Yes, well, the weather was inclement.

AUDELLE. I was just telling the Reverend, for myself, laying my hand upon those prehistoric stones induced a sense of connectedness to the mysterious ancestors of this place, the sheer... force of which I had never experienced before.

BERKELEY. Oh, yes. I have always found it to be a place of dark enchantment. And you, Hannah? Did you experience a... sense of connectedness?

HANNAH. Well, I... I did not remain there for long, so...

Pause.

BERKELEY. You know, I often think of your poor father on nights such as this, Hannah.

HANNAH. I think of him regardless of the day or night.

BERKELEY. He is in your prayers.

HANNAH. With all of my family.

BERKELEY. With all of us. My dear Alice is still alive – in my mind, her fragile bones still shining beneath her transparent skin, just as poor old Edward still lives in yours. He is so strong there. So... real. In which case, how can anyone say he doesn't exist? Of course he still exists! These recent times weigh hard on you, I suspect, Hannah.

HANNAH. Well. I have many blessings. I shouldn't complain.

BERKELEY. Yes, but even good news can bring its difficulties, especially when set against a tragedy so terrible as the one we have witnessed in Jamestown.

HANNAH. Especially when it occurred on the very evening you sought to summon the spirits of the dead.

BERKELEY (*laughs, almost delighted she has risen to the bait*). 'The dead'! We didn't cause those buildings to fall down. Hasn't the Colonel himself said as much. Now, I hope you don't mind, but you will be aware I have learned something of your recent experiences, Hannah.

HANNAH. Yes, well, I don't want to discuss that.

BERKELEY. And I will come straight out with it and say it's a pity you consider the specialness of your gift a burden – when rightly it should be something you ought to cherish. And be grateful for.

HANNAH. I just want to stop it now, so…

BERKELEY. Stop it?! Well, it's my belief that would be a dreadful shame. What you really need is to *understand* it. Yes. You can take the sting of its unknowability away, and we would like to help you.

Pause.

HANNAH. How can you help me?

BERKELEY. Do you know what a… seance is, Hannah?

HANNAH. I have heard of it.

BERKELEY. Yes, on the Continent one hears a lot of rubbish about these matters, I'm afraid. The facts are quite simple. I can explain precisely why you are in your predicament, Audelle?

AUDELLE. It's really quite straightforward.

BERKELEY. Dear me, that's quite a draught. Is that door closed, Audelle?

AUDELLE *goes and shuts the door quietly.*

You see, Hannah, there is only God. (*Pause.*) Nature comes from God. It is a part of God. And man is part of nature. But we are a very special part, because only the human being can know itself and think for itself. Consider a fish or a dog. They are prisoners of their instinct, slaves to nature, where man is free.

HANNAH. No. A dog is freer than a man, if you ask me.

AUDELLE. But a dog cannot choose. No animal can. When it's hungry it will eat, when it's tired it must sleep. Thus it has no choice, correct? But man — a man may *deny* his instinct, *suppress* his appetite and decide for himself what is right or wrong. He is even free to destroy himself!

BERKELEY. Can a dog do that?

AUDELLE. Being conscious means man is both part of nature and yet free of it — all at once.

BERKELEY. You see, it has recently been proven, Hannah, beyond logical denial –

HANNAH *goes to interrupt.*

Beyond logical denial, that with the emergence of the human subject there is finally a part of nature which *knows* itself! Do you understand? All of this, everything around us, and you and I and Audelle –

AUDELLE. And Grandie –

BERKELEY. And Grandie and everything else – this is all… the mind of God awakening and coming to know itself. And when we look at each other, just as I am looking at you now, it is as though God is looking at Himself in a mirror. And each eye, the beholder and the beheld, reflect the other back and forth as mirrors do, into a kind of genuine infinity. The infinity of God. You see? We *are* God… Isn't that wonderful? Now, knowing that we are God is of course a great responsibility but it's not something we want to bandy about!

AUDELLE. Of course not.

BERKELEY. For so long we have all felt cut away from God, somehow seeking 'forgiveness' in order to be reunited. But we were never separate from Him! So you need not feel any guilt, Hannah. Your feelings are holy! And just as in any walk of life we meet people with great gifts, this one a great carpenter, that one a great musician, so you have a great talent, Hannah.

HANNAH. You call it a gift.

AUDELLE. Hannah, your gift is simply consciousness itself. That's right. And so profound is your talent in this case, so acute its perceptiveness, you are capable of beholding not just what is here in this moment, but what is beyond and before time.

BERKELEY. That's all it is! Nothing more! (*Laughs*.) And certainly nothing to fear. So in order to dispel the terror visited upon you by the voices you have perceived here in this house, I want to invite you now, through the medium of a seance, to reconsider them in this light: and thereby uncover the divine within yourself. Here. With us. Now. Tonight. We are here to support you and to help you. Why, even Grandie can take part! All humankind is welcome here! (*Laughs*.)

AUDELLE. A seance is merely a mindful contemplation, Hannah. We... sit together and reflect. That is all.

HANNAH. Will it stop me hearing things?

BERKELEY. I cannot say it will. Indeed I hope it will not! But I will stake my life on it that it will take the fear away. My life!

Pause.

HANNAH. What happens?

BERKELEY. What happens? Why nothing more than were we to open a book and read a story. The book we open is the book of time. The story is the unfolding revelation of God's presence in all things. No more. Thus we may understand who or what has been drawn to this place to seek you out. And armed with this knowledge, it is my firm belief you will progress into your new life with a hitherto unforeseen freedom, for ever.

Pause. HANNAH *is thinking about it.*

AUDELLE. Do not waste your youth as I have, hemmed in on either side by an abyss of fear.

BERKELEY. Release yourself. Permit yourself,

AUDELLE. Forgive yourself.

BERKERLEY. And trust me. Won't you trust me?

HANNAH *coughs.*

Yes, we are all getting that cold!

AUDELLE. Allow me. (*Approaches the drinks.*) Berkeley?

BERKELEY. Water for me, Audelle. Thank you. Look at you, Grandie. So well I remember your charms when you sang before the assembled throng here at Mount Prospect. Your wit. Your gameful eyes so animated with shy promise. Then, as now. Yes, I remember you, Grandie.

AUDELLE *brings a drink of brandy to* HANNAH.

AUDELLE. Sip this, Miss Hannah.

BERKELEY. Yes, a sip to clear the lungs. Well done, Audelle.

HANNAH *drinks while* AUDELLE *takes his bottle of laudanum from his pocket. He thumps his chest.*

AUDELLE. I think I need to loosen my…

Coughs lightly and indicates the bottle to HANNAH. *She holds out her glass, he pours some laudanum into her brandy and she drinks it.*

BERKELEY. Yes, Grandie. (*Holds out his hand to her.*) How you would dance the young men to a defeated collapse!

GRANDIE *reaches towards* BERKELEY *uncertainly, but then withdraws her hand.*

Yes, long ago… (*Takes a cord with a crucifix, some feathers and stones strung along it, placing it round his neck like a necklace.*) How silent is the darkness tonight. You may take my hand, Grandie. Take her hand, Hannah. She is your anchor. There is great love there still. (*Pause.*) Do not be afraid. Who else has ever offered to help you as we do? Take her hand, she loves you.

HANNAH *takes* GRANDIE'*s hand.* GRANDIE *gives her other hand to* BERKELEY. AUDELLE *takes* BERKELEY'*s hand.*

Let us pray. (*With pained concentration.*) Lord God, unknowable father, while we struggle oftbetimes to comprehend thy wishes, forgive us – sinners as we are – as we fulsomely seek to know thy bidding. Bless us here tonight. Protect us as darkness falls through the world and we gather in Your name to wish our daughter Hannah a peaceful existence, replete with spiritual calm. We are beset at every turn with temptations, with dire puzzles which would draw us from Your path and hide the light that might show us to Your dwelling where our true home awaits. Lord, shield us with the blanket of Your forgiveness, Lord…

Sound of a window rattling in the house somewhere.

GRANDIE *takes her hand from* BERKELEY'*s.*

(*Firmly.*) Grandie… (*More gently.*) Grandie. Let us say our bedtime prayers, come on now. That's it…

HANNAH. Perhaps we have done enough for now, Berkeley.

BERKELEY. We are merely saying a prayer, Hannah. Let us pray. Let us pray.

GRANDIE *looks at* HANNAH. HANNAH *returns her gaze.* BERKELEY *takes* GRANDIE'*s hand.*

Lord, as you peer into the rags of our pitiful souls, grant us safety here, to cleanse our house. To liberate the daughter of our house. (*Pause.*) To all else who lurk here, I say unto you now – in the name of God – reveal yourselves and submit to our instruction to quit this place. No longer disturb this girl. She may hear you while all else fall deaf to your pleas, but we shall not brook that you harass her with your infernal concerns!

They hear something move, like furniture being dragged across a room above them.

Ignore it! (*Bellows.*) In the name of Our Lord, Jesus Christ...

AUDELLE. Quieter, Berkeley...

BERKELEY. I'm sorry. (*Lowers his volume.*) In the name of Our Lord, Jesus Christ, our saviour, the one true God who became man to know death as man knows it, for love of His children, I command thee – come forward and go. (*Pause.*) Come forward and show yourself!

Again something moves somewhere, a dull thud.

Ignore it. I command thee, cold spirit. Show thyself. Submit thyself. *Credo. Credo. Credo. Credo in Unum Deum, Patrem omnipotentem, factorem caeli et terrae, visibilium omnium et invisibilium.*

HANNAH *coughs.*

Deus meus ex toto corde paenitet me morum peccatorum...

HANNAH*'s body shudders.*

Credo... Credo... Credo...

HANNAH (*suddenly starts singing in a strident voice while her eyes are closed*). Oh, the green moss grows upon the heather where the briar grows upon the wood...

BERKELEY *falls silent.* AUDELLE *and* BERKELEY *look at each other.*

BERKELEY. *Non solum poenas a te juste statutes promeritus sum...*

HANNAH (*sings*). My love is sleeping in the bower where a lonely graveyard stood. She sings of an ancient flower... She sings of an ancient flower...

BERKELEY....*Adiuvante gratia tua, de cetero me no peccaridique occasiones proximas fugiturum...*

HANNAH (*sings*). She sings... (*Her song peters out.*)

GRANDIE (*casually*). He knew my name.

BERKELEY. Shh... Grandie.

HANNAH *looks at* BERKELEY. *She speaks gently and calmly, her eyes seeing beyond him into somewhere else.*

HANNAH. Have you seen it?

Pause.

BERKELEY. Have we seen what?

HANNAH (*gently*). The infant.

BERKELEY. What infant?

HANNAH. The baby... that was here.

Pause.

AUDELLE. Berkeley...

BERKELEY. Yes, yes... (*To* HANNAH.) Who speaks? (*Pause.*) Who speaks?

HANNAH....Shh! Listen... (*Pause.*) Where is it!?

BERKELEY. Where is what? (*Short pause.*) We hear nothing.

HANNAH. Sh... (*Pause.*) Listen...

HANNAH *suddenly stands up. She looks at the others.*

BERKELEY. Who are you that speaks through this girl?

HANNAH. You can't hear it.

BERKELEY. Are you Edward come to us?

HANNAH. I can hear her.

She looks round the room.

BERKELEY. Do you hear your daughter, Edward? (*Pause.*) Are you Edward? (*Pause.*) You know you must leave here. You must quit this place. You can no longer remain.

HANNAH. But how can I leave?

BERKELEY. You are called to join your Creator. You died here, Edward. You cannot stay.

HANNAH. I cannot go. I will see my child.

BERKELEY. You can no longer see your child, Edward, because you died here. (*Pause.*) You died here.

HANNAH. It was a girl, wasn't it?

She walks round the room, as though looking for something.

BERKELEY. Who was a girl? (*Pause.*) Speak!

HANNAH. I can hear her crying!

Pause.

BERKELEY. Are you Edward Lambroke? Are you he that took his life in this room?

HANNAH. They've locked me in! They've locked me in!

BERKELEY. Well, you must leave in the name of God.

HANNAH. This is a dream. This must be a dream.

She looks desperately round the room. BERKELEY *follows her.*

BERKELEY. We abide only in the dream of our great Creator, in whose name I command you now to go.

HANNAH. No! They must show me my child.

BERKELEY. You must leave this house in the name of Jesus Christ.

HANNAH. Can you not hear it? Are you made of stone? (*Shouts*.) Can you not hear her?!

AUDELLE. Berkeley…!

BERKELEY (*holding her*). Listen no, no, no, listen, Edward. Are you Edward? You are Edward.

HANNAH. I am Hannah.

BERKELEY. No, you are not. Not Hannah.

GRANDIE. She is Hannah.

HANNAH. I am Hannah Lambroke, and I will not be told I cannot see my child!!

BERKELEY. Shhh…

AUDELLE. She will wake the house!

HANNAH *goes towards the conservatory door and tries the handle*. BERKELEY *blocks her way, she pushes against him*.

BERKELEY. I command whoever torments this girl to leave.

HANNAH. Unlock this door. I demand to see my child.

BERKELEY. Shh… Shh… Hannah, it's alright. Some help please here, Audelle.

AUDELLE *goes to assist* BERKELEY, *restraining* HANNAH.

HANNAH. I will see my child! I will hold my child!

GRANDIE *is agitated by the disruption. She lets out a cry and moves towards the hallway door.*

AUDELLE. Get her out of it, Berkeley! Get her out of it!

HANNAH. Are you mad?! Are you people mad!?

She turns and thumps AUDELLE *around the head and chest until he releases her. He tumbles backwards into the furniture and on to the floor.*

What kind of people are you that you would do such a thing?

She stands glaring at them.

BERKELEY. Hannah. Hannah. It's me. It's Berkeley. Why, we were just praying... ha ha ha... Let's have a little prayer.

HANNAH. I will not pray with you.

BERKELEY. Well, that's alright. That's alright. You just got a fright, that's all. No need for alarm. That's it. We were just...

HANNAH. Don't touch me.

BERKELEY. No, no. I won't... Here, take a drink of water, now shush...

AUDELLE *has backed away towards the hall door near* GRANDIE. HANNAH *goes to the fireplace, her head on her hands on the mantel.* BERKELEY *tries to cajole her with a glass of water. He has his back to* AUDELLE *as the door opens.* AUDELLE *turns to face the music, expecting to see* MADELEINE, *but a very small* CHILD *with a pale face and dark eyes stands looking at* AUDELLE *for a moment before turning and leaving in the gloom.* AUDELLE *stands frozen, looking at the empty doorway.* GRANDIE *is watching* AUDELLE. BERKELEY, *preoccupied with* HANNAH, *sees nothing.*

That's it. That's alright. Sit down...

HANNAH *sits down, her head in her hands.*

AUDELLE *looks at* GRANDIE *who is staring at* AUDELLE. *She suddenly opens her mouth wide and starts screaming at* AUDELLE. AUDELLE *flinches.* GRANDIE *laughs at him, opening her mouth and screaming at him, terrifying him, as though she knows he has just seen a ghost and is mocking him. She hits him with a stick.*

Grandie, shush! Grandie... now... Grandie! What did you do to her?

AUDELLE. What? I... I...

GRANDIE *screams at* AUDELLE *as* MADELEINE *rushes in carrying a candle.*

Pause.

MADELEINE. What in the name of God is happening in here?

BERKELEY. Grandie has... become a little overwrought.

Pause.

MADELEINE. Grandie. That's enough. Hannah. What happened?

BERKELEY (*quickly removing his necklace*). She's just exhausted. We all are. This last week has taken such a considerable toll on all of us.

MADELEINE. What are you talking about?

MRS GOULDING *appears in her nightdress.*

MRS GOULDING. Was someone at the door?

MADELEINE. No, Mrs Goulding. Kindly take Grandie to bed. It's time everyone retired.

MRS GOULDING. Come, Grandie.

GRANDIE *goes to* AUDELLE *and pinches his cheek.*

AUDELLE. Get off me!

MADELEINE. Grandie! Go to bed!

GRANDIE *leaves, followed by* MRS GOULDING.

MRS GOULDING. Grandie, wait for the candle!

Pause.

MADELEINE. What happened?

BERKELEY. Why, nothing! (*Short pause.*) Ha, ha, ha...

MADELEINE. What were you doing?

BERKELEY. Nothing! We were all just discussing the...
horrific events of the past few days. And how upsetting it's
been... and Grandie just...

MADELEINE. Hannah?

HANNAH. I need to lie down.

MADELEINE. Well, get yourself to bed.

HANNAH. Yes, Mama.

MADELEINE. You're shaking.

BERKELEY. That's a dreadful cold that's been going round.

HANNAH *readies herself to leave. She looks at*
BERKELEY *and* AUDELLE. *Behind* MADELEINE*'s back,*
BERKELEY *puts his finger to his lips, begging* HANNAH*'s*
silence.

We will all talk in the morning.

Pause.

MADELEINE. You will pack your bags tomorrow. There will
be too little time on Saturday.

BERKELEY. Yes. We will all pack tomorrow. (*Pause.*) Yes.

HANNAH *leaves.*

MADELEINE *looks at* BERKELEY. *He gives her a little*
smile.

What can I say? Goodnight, Madeleine.

She looks at AUDELLE.

MADELEINE. And what's the matter with you now, Mr
Audelle? Too much or too little brandy?

She leaves. Pause.

BERKELEY. Well! Intriguing! (*Wipes his brow with a handkerchief.*) What did you make of that?! Are you alright, Audelle? You look ghastly.

AUDELLE. Yes, I'm… I'm fine.

BERKELEY. She was… I mean, we were really in the presence of something, weren't we?

AUDELLE. Yes.

BERKELEY. My word. The very air crackles. What did we unleash?

AUDELLE *doesn't answer.*

Come, we must abed. I would not anger our hostess a moment more.

AUDELLE. I will follow you.

BERKELEY *pauses.*

Please, Berkeley. I need a moment.

BERKELEY. Alright, well… Do not stay too late.

AUDELLE. No.

BERKELEY. And no more brandy. Or medicine. Come now. Directly.

BERKELEY *takes a candle and leaves.* AUDELLE *sits on the arm of a chair looking at the spot where he saw the* CHILD.

The lights darken and he leaves as the room brightens again, bringing us to the next day, Friday May 24th. It is late afternoon, between 5 and 6 p.m. The first bare fade of dusk is in the sky. CLARE *is changing candles and lighting new ones. She throws the old stubs in a cloth bag to be reused downstairs.* FINGAL *comes in through the conservatory. He opens the tall double doors and trips, almost falling into the room, dropping the rifle he carries and startling* CLARE. *He has a swollen black eye.*

CLARE. Mr Fingal!

FINGAL (*drunkenly putting a finger to his lips*). Aye aye aye…
(*Looking at where he lost his footing.*) Someone needs to fix
those floorboards.

CLARE (*resuming her work*). There's nothing wrong with the
floorboards.

FINGAL *props his rifle against a wall and stands in the
room seemingly devoid of purpose, drink having reduced his
worries to an unreachable drone within his head*

FINGAL. Miss me?

CLARE. Why would I miss you?

FINGAL. Because… I've been gone.

CLARE. You always turn up. Where were you? Down in
Jamestown, I suppose?

FINGAL. And if I was?

CLARE. Look at you. What happened to your eye?

FINGAL. A bat flew into it.

CLARE. A bat?

FINGAL. I was… coming up, down the road, up out of
Jamestown and – kablammo! Right in the kisser.

CLARE. Yes, well wait until the others see you.

FINGAL. Nobody can see me, Clare. I'm like a ghost now.

CLARE. You will be a ghost the way you're going.

Pause. He watches her work.

FINGAL. They found another little one this morning. In the
rubble. An infant.

CLARE. Yes, I heard.

FINGAL. That's seven little ones.

CLARE. Yes, I heard already, Mr Fingal.

FINGAL. Alright, Jesus Christ! I'm only telling you. Pss.

He goes to pour himself a drink.

A bloody death hole is all it was. Still, roof over your head. (*Gloomily.*) All warm in together. (*Drinks.*) So, look, I'll have my money soon. When the dowry comes in. Thirteen months' wages, I'm owed. What do you think of that? That's when the pressure comes off. (*Pause.*) And given time, perhaps even I will be forgiven.

CLARE. Forgiven what?

FINGAL. Even you'll forgive me.

CLARE. What's to forgive? Except how you would kill your own kindness.

FINGAL. Kindness? What kindness?

CLARE. Don't act the criminal, Mr Fingal. I have seen it.

FINGAL. Where? In those whispers I stuck in your ear, so full of grog and poitín you had to hold me up in the darkness of the laneway?

CLARE. I have seen it.

Pause.

FINGAL. So anyway… Clare… Em… Can you loan me some money?

CLARE. Pardon?

FINGAL. Can you loan me some money, just until… I am in debt.

CLARE. For how much?

FINGAL. Fifty-five guineas.

CLARE. Fifty-five guineas! From playing cards!?

FINGAL. I will sign a promissory letter this very day and endeavour to have you reimbursed within the month, or when the dowry for Miss Hannah arrives, whichever is sooner.

CLARE. I have but two guineas in the world.

FINGAL. Two guineas will suffice for today.

CLARE. I can't.

FINGAL. Why not?

CLARE. It is for my passage to Ontario.

FINGAL (*disparaging*). You're not going to Ontario, Clare...

CLARE. When her ladyship and Hannah move to Northampton I will be left with no employment. What will I do without my passage?

FINGAL. But you will get your money back!

CLARE. No. My father would kill me.

FINGAL. He'll never know!

CLARE. He holds my money for me!

FINGAL. You can get it. Tell him something. What? Would you betray me to him?

CLARE. Of course not, but...

FINGAL. Then it's settled! I will bring you a letter tonight that will ease your mind. It's as good as money, I promise you. When Miss Hannah's dowry arrives, madam will settle her debts, you will have your two guineas, I'll pay the balance of what I owe in Jamestown, and we'll all...

He raises his hands in conclusion. Pause.

CLARE. Would you not... consider going away?

FINGAL. Where? (*Disparaging.*) To Canada? Come on...

CLARE. Or anywhere. Away. Away from the trouble in your nature that drags you down again and again to Jamestown. Away. Imagine a clean country. Your own little place with a fire dying in the hearth and a good meal inside you and the peacefulness maybe of knowing that your… wife or your… your child is soundly asleep nearby.

FINGAL. How can you hold out hope like that? Ha? Even for me?

CLARE. I don't know. I just see it.

FINGAL. You see a dream.

CLARE. If you like.

FINGAL. Yeah, well I don't believe in dreams.

He takes a drink.

CLARE (*sharply*). Well, ask her ladyship to loan you the money then! She likes you personally, isn't that what you're always saying?

FINGAL (*moving to quieten her voice*). Don't be ridiculous!

CLARE. Yeah? Well, I saw her here one morning talking to a soldier just out there on the stairs.

FINGAL. What soldier?

CLARE. Some soldier. At the top of the stairs just before it got bright. She never saw me.

FINGAL. From the garrison?

CLARE. No, he wasn't a rough-looking one at all. He had a fancy uniform.

FINGAL. Well, that's… What are you talking about? Can you see in the dark now?

CLARE. Why? Are you jealous? It's so clear how you think of her.

FINGAL. Don't talk nonsense, girl…

CLARE. You do. And you say you don't believe in dreams! Huh! You dream the most of any of us, Mr Fingal.

FINGAL (*loudly*). Will you shut the hell up, I said! (*Pause*.) I'll give you a dream. Before any of you were awake, the other morning, I beat the boy out in the yard. You didn't see that, did you?

CLARE. Little James Furay?

FINGAL. Yes, little James. You didn't see it because I did it before anybody was up. I woke him in the dark and I said, 'Get down here with me to the stables.' He rose without a question, rubbing his eyes, and I got him in there and I made him wash with cold water from the pail and then I said, 'What do you mean, sir, having two lame horses in your charge?' 'What?' he says. 'Take off your shirt,' says I, 'I'm to whip you for what's happened to her ladyship's horse.'

CLARE. When was this?

FINGAL. The morning after we went to Jamestown to see the ruins. Out there by the stable. And do you know what he did? He just went over to the corner and took off his jacket and his shirt and he stood there before me. This boy who's lived with me in the lodge since he was seven years old. His skinny white body, so small for his age, and his eyes so trusting and innocent and I took a whip and I turned him round and belted him so hard I stripped half the skin off his back and he couldn't get his shirt back on. His hands were too shaky anyway, so I threw his jacket round his shoulders and told him to piss off back down to the lodge.

Pause.

CLARE. Why would you do such a thing?

FINGAL. Because her ladyship told me to.

CLARE. She told you to do that to him?

FINGAL. She told me to get to the bottom of what happened to the horses.

CLARE. But, Mr Fingal…

FINGAL. I know. I know! Do you think I don't know?! (*Pause*.) I went down to Jamestown and played cards for three days and nights. I ended up in a fight over my debts and curled up in a ditch and prayed for God to punish me. But He knew, you see. He knew it would be worse to leave me alone.

CLARE. Where is the boy?

FINGAL (*shrugs*). In the gate lodge.

CLARE. On his own?

FINGAL. We must make… that assumption. Can you let me have some money tonight, Clare? Anything that I could just bring down to…

The door opens. MADELEINE *comes in with* GRANDIE. CLARE *resumes her work and* FINGAL *puts down his drink.*

MADELEINE. Clare, will you please go and see if Hannah is still in the chapel? She has a cold and I want her to come in.

CLARE. Yes, madam.

MADELEINE. And come straight back as Mrs Goulding will need you.

CLARE. Yes, madam.

CLARE *goes.*

MADELEINE. Mr Fingal.

FINGAL. Madam.

MADELEINE. What happened to your face?

FINGAL. An altercation regarding a personal matter which has not nor will not interfere with my professional duties.

MADELEINE. You have been in Jamestown, I take it?

FINGAL. Yes.

Pause.

MADELEINE. What say folk?

FINGAL. Regarding...?

MADELEINE. Regarding the collapse of my properties.

FINGAL. They say such is the lot of the poor.

MADELEINE. To suffer the rich.

FINGAL. They suffer themselves. They should better themselves.

MADELEINE. As you have bettered yourself.

FINGAL. As you see.

There is a short pause, and he starts to leave, forgetting his rifle.

Well, good evening.

MADELEINE. We are gathering to say farewell to the Reverend and Mr Audelle. And to wish Hannah a good journey. You may join us, Mr Fingal, should you feel up to it.

FINGAL. Thank you, madam.

MADELEINE. But may I suggest you go to the kitchen and tidy yourself up.

FINGAL. Yes, madam.

MADELEINE. And drink some tea.

FINGAL. Yes, madam.

MADELEINE. Oh, and Mr Fingal.

He halts.

Where is the boy? (*Pause.*) Where is James Furay?

BERKELEY *comes in.*

BERKELEY. Ah, Fingal! The very man. Oh dear me, that is a shiner! What happened? Are you alright?

FINGAL. A hunting accident, sir.

BERKELEY. Oh dear, well, actually, I was going to ask you. We leave tomorrow around noon, but say if I were up at five or so, could I get a pony to go down in the glen to see if I can bag a wood pigeon or two?

FINGAL. Yes, sir.

BERKELEY. I heard there were a few about.

FINGAL. Yes, sir, I'll see about a pony.

BERKELEY. Only if it's no trouble.

FINGAL. No, sir, I'll see to it personally.

BERKELEY. Thanks, Fingal.

FINGAL. Yes, sir.

BERKELEY. And don't let me go without giving you a little… eh… (*Signals a monetary tip.*)

FINGAL *nods uncomfortably and leaves.*

Poor old Fingal. Fond of the drop, I take it.

MADELEINE. No more so than the rest of his family.

BERKELEY. Mmm. Well, Grandie! We gather to say farewell – until Northampton.

GRANDIE *just returns his gaze steadily, giving him the slightest of smiles.*

MADELEINE. Yes.

BERKELEY. Madeleine. I am sorry if I disturbed you when I entered your chamber this morning. I could never have forgiven myself had I awoken to hear sobbing and had done nothing to at least to investigate.

MADELEINE. I was quite alright, thank you. It was just a bad dream.

BERKELEY. Well, it must have been very bad. May I?

He goes to the drinks.

MADELEINE. Not for me

GRANDIE. Good morning, McMickins.

MADELEINE. But a small drop for Grandie if you don't mind.

BERKELEY. Grandie, of course… I know these have been such trying days, Madeleine. Do not think I could possibly be unaware of that. My affection for you is unassailable, for you see, to me – perhaps unfortunately for you – you will always be the little child who would follow me about on my summer visits here as a young man.

MADELEINE. Oh, come, I never followed you about.

BERKELEY. No, no, you did. You were probably too young to remember. You showed such delight when we fished for trout in the lake. She was like my little sister, wasn't she, Grandie? And you still are. So when I heard you sobbing down the corridor in the darkness before dawn this morning, how could I not at least venture forth to offer you my comfort in the gloom? However, if you don't mind me saying, that you would refuse my presence with such vehemence and unexpected bad language quite unnerved me. I hardly slept after I crept back to my bed.

MADELEINE. I regret that your feelings were not spared, Berkeley, but I simply have no time for your perceived hardships at present, I'm sorry.

BERKELEY. You are growing old, Madeleine. I am already old. Mark you, even at fifty, one is very old. These years, between now and fifty – settle your affairs, dear.

MADELEINE. I am settling my affairs.

BERKELEY. Yes, your earthly affairs.

MADELEINE. Oh, Berkeley, please, I'm too tired.

BERKELEY. I mean to speak plainly with you, Madeleine, because I love you and I only want what is for the best. A sickness of denial and illusion pervades here in this room, in this very room you so boldly use. But you will not let me help you.

MADELEINE. But I don't want your help!

BERKELEY. Madeleine, I know you can see the things Hannah has experienced here. You deny your gift in order to embrace your delusion that Edward actually departed the night he ended his life here. It is my firm belief he did not depart.

MADELEINE. Berkeley, I swear I will brain you with this poker if you keep on at me, do you hear me? What were you doing in here with Hannah last night?

BERKELEY. I was assisting her, Madeleine! I was helping a girl who has endured the unimaginable strain of being the sole recipient of a communication from the beyond, with no one to believe her or help her to interpret it.

MADELEINE. Oh!

BERKELEY. The spirit realm flows through this place like a river! It always has! This is the very place that piqued my interest in everything that ever led to my downfall and my disgrace, but I don't regret it. Not for a second. Audelle is sensate. And he can feel it. I know him. And I know he can barely keep his mind together, so strong is its current!

MADELEINE. I would contend that Mr Audelle struggles to keep his mind together under the calmest of circumstances! Are you not ashamed to consort with someone with a reputation such as his? Let alone invite him into my house to instruct my daughter?

BERKELEY (*sadly*). Oh, my child…

MADELEINE. I'm not your child, Berkeley. You *are* old, I don't deny it. Age has racked your body, but it is your brain that has suffered most! I hear you speak and I believe you are like a man with an infant's toy box in his head.

GRANDIE. Woah!

BERKELEY (*shocked and angry*). Madeleine!

MADELEINE. Yes! You may say you have always regarded me as your sister, but in truth when I was a child I always thought you were an embarrassing buffoon and I was never anything less than utterly fatigued by your boring theories. I had assumed life's experience might mould you into a more agreeable person; however, I am confounded by your undeniable mental degeneration. In my opinion, mere vanity has convinced you of your holy vocation and I was not in the least part surprised you managed to get yourself defrocked! To say nothing of the unspeakable strain it must have caused your poor Alice! And while we are speaking plainly, may I say I find the fact that you are still one of Lord Ashby's spiritual advisors only makes me wonder should I worry more for his soul or his sanity!

BERKELEY. I see.

MADELEINE. None of this means I don't love you, Berkeley. And I am grateful for your introduction to Lord Ashby, but the sooner we deliver Hannah from your orbit and into the shelter of her new life in Northampton, the happier I will be.

BERKELEY. We will all be in the same orbit in Northampton, Madeleine, supping from the same well.

MADELEINE. You will not get past me again, Berkeley. And I will outlast you.

BERKELEY. Yes, perhaps I stand on the threshold of forever's mysterious twilight while you still reside in life's bright room of vitality where all appears commodious, but you cannot fool a fool. I have heard you – crying in the night, while you push away the hand that would help you.

MADELEINE. I cried while I slept! I was dreaming about those poor souls who lost their lives crowded into a dreadful terrace in Jamestown I had scarcely ever thought about! I cried at my own powerlessness and selfishness seeing how they had lived and died! What do you want me to say?

BERKELEY. Madeleine, we all heard it.

MADELEINE. Heard what?

BERKELEY. The great clap of thunder here – in this room – the night those wretches perished. Their pain was manifest here in that moment, surely to God, and yet you deny it. You see it all, Madeleine, I know you do. You, Grandie, your poor mother, Hannah, all of you have a shared capacity to apprehend the beyond. And you perhaps more than any of them have the darkest instinct for second sight.

MADELEINE. No, Berkeley.

BERKELEY. Do not lie! Your gift is the most intense! That is why you deny it the hardest. And you lie so badly because greater the lie the deeper the pain! What is it about this place that it is such a conduit for desperate souls? Don't you care to know!?

MADELEINE. No I don't! Because there was always pain here at Mount Prospect! It was here before us and will be here after we are gone!

BERKELEY. But Hannah cannot endure it, can she? Nor could Edward. Yet while he sought the sweet embrace of the final escape, he never got out, did he!

MADELEINE. Oh, he got out. And yet he lives. And he will live wherever I live as long as I am alive. But not because he is trapped. What lives is my knowledge that what happened to him was all a stupid mistake. It was a mistake, but every single I day I believe I might somehow reach out and correct it — but I can't! Don't you see that? I can't!

There is a knock at the door.

Yes?

CLARE *appears at the door.*

CLARE. Excuse me, madam, Mrs Goulding has asked may we start to lay the table?

MADELEINE. Yes. Of course. Thank you, Clare.

CLARE. Yes, madam.

CLARE *leaves.* MADELEINE *crumples, taking a moment to compose herself.* BERKELEY *looks on uncertainly.*

BERKELEY. But, Madeleine, it was not your fault. I... I had no idea that you... Well, I... Don't cry my dear.

MADELEINE. You see, the day he did it I had simply lost patience. I told him all of the things I had often thought but never uttered. They exploded from me in such a fusillade of bitter release, still do I see the expression of pain and helplessness in his face. I was young and ignorant! Perhaps I felt it would galvanise him or change him. I know now, of course, that he was ill. Neither of us understood that the imbalance in his mind required real care. All I managed to do that morning was strike out at him and add to his worries. After I had done it, something in me knew I shouldn't leave him alone. But something else, something so angry and evil, *allowed* me to abandon him while I stormed off down the laneways round the back of the garden in the cold afternoon. My temper rose and grew and ate itself until it was sick of itself and sick of me and until it was as though there was no one left inside me any more. And when I got back... he had done it. He was gone. Hannah was down in the kitchen with Mrs Goulding eating spoonfuls of honey. She found him, you know that, don't you. (*Tearfully for a moment.*) Poor old Mike Wallace had had to lift him down! (*Regaining composure.*) I don't know what Edward perceived here that drove him from us, Berkeley, but it will not happen to my daughter. I'm not like you. I do not search for voices or shadows because I have never had to look very hard in order to find them. Perhaps I have never had your faith in the goodness of God's order, Berkeley. But then again, you see, I have never had your pig-headed immaturity either. That's simply how I have to see it.

MRS GOULDING *rings a bell in the hallway.*

Take your drink, Berkeley. Mrs Goulding is bringing the refreshments. I insist Hannah's last evening here be an easy and gay affair. It's the least she deserves.

BERKELEY. Well, of course.

MADELEINE. I'm warning you, Berkeley.

BERKELEY. I am the soul of joviality.

The door is opened by MRS GOULDING. CLARE *carries a large tray and* FINGAL *carries a bowl of hot punch, using napkins to protect his hands from the heat. Dusk is gathering and this scene gradually darkens.* FINGAL *is unsteady and spills some punch.* CLARE *goes to wipe it.*

Mrs Goulding's hot punch.

MRS GOULDING. Most certainly. I have it, I have it. (*Wipes up the drops.*) Scones on the mat, hot punch on the trivet, Mr Fingal.

BERKELEY. I trust you have been as moderate as ever with the rum?

MRS GOULDING. I would say I have been judicious.

BERKELEY. In that case, a measure for our generous hostess, quickly, Clare.

MADELEINE. Please, tend to yourselves first.

BERKELEY. No, no, a dram, Madeleine. Let us dispel the evening gloom. Thank you, Clare. That's right.

CLARE *helps* MRS GOULDING *fetch drinks for* MADELEINE *and* GRANDIE.

MADELEINE. Clare. Did you find Hannah?

CLARE. Yes, madam. She is changing in her room.

MADELEINE. Will you tell her we are waiting for her to come down, please?

CLARE. Yes, madam.

MADELEINE. Thank you, Clare.

As CLARE *goes,* AUDELLE *enters.*

BERKELEY. Ah, Mr Audelle's nose for impending hospitality remains impeccable.

AUDELLE. Yes, well, good evening. It's a lucky thing you rang that bell, Mrs Goulding. I was positively pole-axed up there in my room. You make those beds far too comfortably, I'm afraid. Is that tea.

BERKELEY. Well, this will wake you up.

FINGAL *brings a drink for* AUDELLE.

AUDELLE. Oh, thank you.

MRS GOULDING. This hot rum punch was a recipe given me by my grandmother and has been the requisite post-hunting libation here at Mount Prospect for at least fifty years or more.

BERKELEY. You get a sniff of that, Audelle? It's not the gut-rot that you quaff by the pint in Chapelgate.

MRS GOULDING. On one famous occasion in 1797, a shout went up while sixty waited to dine: 'Forgo the meal,' they cried, having downed a barrel of this grog, 'Our thirst has eclipsed our appetite!' And nothing would do only except for me to go back down in the scullery – somewhat unsteadily myself – to mount a fresh barrel upon the fire.

BERKELEY. In the golden days here at Mount Prospect. The Earl in all his splendour yet. Grandie in gracious repose. The stories the Earl would regale us with — how his great-grandfather survived to see his one hundred and six living descendants, borne of four wives...

MRS GOULDING. 'And each uglier than the last.'

BERKELEY (*simultaneously*). 'And each more ugly than the last!'

HANNAH *enters with* CLARE.

MRS GOULDING. Miss Hannah may be glad her mother's line is in a straight descent from the early batch!

BERKELEY. The fresh flowers!

MADELEINE. You speak of my family, Mrs Goulding.

MRS GOULDING. Psh! They are practically my family too, madam, may I be so bold.

BERKELEY. Yes, where would Mount Prospect be without good old Mrs Goulding?

MRS GOULDING. I wonder!

BERKELEY. And Mr Fingal, of course. Remember, Fingal, those endless afternoons on the lawn, you were but a garsoon – and two or three summers in a row, if I'm not mistaken. When you were only ten or eleven. You followed that girl round and round.

MRS GOULDING. Oh yes!

BERKELEY. We talked of it so much and laughed so often! Your little moon-face behind her – her nut-brown hair always tied up in a white ribbon. Remember? She was perhaps a year or two older than you – who was she?

MRS GOULDING. She was the daughter of old Mr McElligot who used run the stables back then.

BERKELEY. Oh yes! Kate McElligot! And Fingal would follow behind her, follow her, follow her, while we all dined on blankets on the lawn. A hundred guests or more – until one day she finally turned round, in front of all of us and said, 'Will you leave me be, Fingal, or I'll break your feet to halt you!'

MRS GOULDING (*simultaneously*). '...I'll break your feet to halt you!' Yes...

They laugh.

BERKELEY. Do you remember? We were all in earshot and everybody laughed! Whatever happened to her?

Short pause.

FINGAL. She married my brother.

BERKELEY. Oh, yes. (*Beat.*) Yes... Yes. A lovely girl. (*Pause.*) Who will give us a song? Hannah?

HANNAH. I have a cold, Berkeley.

BERKELEY. A quiet song?

HANNAH *shakes her head.*

Oh, who will sing? Mrs Goulding?

MRS GOULDING. Oh dear me, no – it's far too early for me. Clare will sing.

BERKELEY. Do you sing, Clare?

MADELEINE. She has a sweet voice.

CLARE. Oh, I don't know!

BERKELEY. Oh, please do!

MRS GOULDING. Here, get yourself another dram of punch and Miss Hannah might play the piano for you?

BERKELEY. Oh, say you will. She will! I will pour you a dram. (*He takes* CLARE's *glass.*) Hannah, please play for her.

CLARE. I have not sang for so long.

BERKELEY. No matter! No matter! What better reason not to refuse? Here, drink this. Hannah, what will you play?

MRS GOULDING. 'As I Roved Out'?

BERKELEY. Oh yes, so beautiful. Come listen to this, Audelle.

CLARE and HANNAH *look at each other in silent agreement.* CLARE *takes a drink and* HANNAH *goes to the piano and starts to play a simple accompaniment. She looks round at* CLARE.

CLARE. Oh my God…!

She laughs nervously and presently begins singing a plaintive rendition of an old ballad.

(*Sings.*)
    I dreamed I roamed on a bright May morning
    To view the meadows and flowers gay
    Whom should I spy but my own true lover
    As she sat under yon willow tree
    I took off my hat and I did salute her
    I did salute her most courageously
    When she turned around, well the tears fell from her
    Saying 'False young man you have deluded me…'
    At night I wake in my bed of slumber
    Thoughts of my love running in my mind
    As I turn around to embrace my darling
    Only darkness and grief do I find
    And I wish the Queen would call home her army
    From the West Indies, Amerikay and Spain
    And every man to his wedded woman
    In hope that you and I will meet again.

As the song ends, she is crying, as is MRS GOULDING. HANNAH *sits quietly at the piano.* FINGAL *looks at the floor.* GRANDIE *leads the applause.*

MRS GOULDING. Isn't that lovely?

BERKELEY. Dear me. I am quite overcome now! Well done, Clare.

CLARE. I'm sorry, I… (*Dabs at her eyes.*)

BERKELEY. No, no. Such depth of emotion is only appropriate.

MADELEINE. That was beautiful, Clare.

CLARE. I'm sorry, madam.

MADELEINE *smiles reassuringly.*

BERKELEY. Has anyone lighter fare? Hannah?

HANNAH *shakes her head.*

One more song in your parlour?

HANNAH. I can't, no, I'm sorry.

GRANDIE (*suddenly sings with confidence*).

> While the green moss grows upon the heather,
>   The briar grows upon the wood,
>   My love lies sleeping in a bower,
>   Where a lonely graveyard stood...

She applauds herself. The others clap.

BERKELEY. Thank you, Grandie.

MRS GOULDING. Very nice, Grandie.

HANNAH. Em... I just wanted to... em...

BERKELEY. Hannah...

HANNAH. Firstly, I wanted to thank everyone for all your efforts in the last few days. And thank Berkeley and Mr Audelle for travelling all this way to chaperone me and Mrs Goulding for making so many arrangements for my departure. And thank you, Mother, for putting my future so firmly at the centre of your concerns. However, something has happened to convince me that... I... I have decided... that I cannot go.

Pause.

BERKELEY (*with a slightly sickened laugh*). Hannah...

HANNAH. I am sorry and I want to apologise to everyone, but my mind has been made up and I feel unable to fulfil my commitment. I'm sorry.

She looks at MADELEINE. MADELEINE *looks down. All is silent.*

FINGAL. But she has to.

MRS GOULDING. Mr Fingal…

Pause.

FINGAL. She has to!

BERKELEY. Alright, Fingal…

FINGAL. Everything is arranged! This is… I mean… (*Laughs as though this just can't be happening.*) What are we going to do?

MADELEINE. Mr Fingal, we can discuss this later.

FINGAL (*points at* AUDELLE). No. No, hold on a minute. This is him. Isn't it? Yes, you.

AUDELLE. I beg your pardon?

FINGAL. They were supposed to escort her to her new home and settle the advancement of the estate, but they brought the undoing of the whole venture within them.

MADELEINE. Not now, Mr Fingal…

FINGAL. What?

MADELEINE. Not now!

CLARE. Willie…

FINGAL. Don't you 'not now' me, madam, now, not now, not now! (*To* AUDELLE.) Yous were seen. They were seen! You think we know nothing of your reputation, Mr Audelle? You come here with the Reverend, your heads bowed and your hands clasped together, but nothing is holy. I've heard all about you down in Jamestown, ha? Ha? What were they doing up at the Queen's Tomb?

MADELEINE. What?

FINGAL. Ask them that!

MADELEINE. When?

FINGAL. The other evening. When they were abroad on one of their nature walks.

AUDELLE. I may assure you, sir...!

FINGAL. No. You can't assure me. You were seen, sir. You were seen.

BERKELEY. What was seen? What are you talking about?

FINGAL. Miss Hannah was seen, running, and tears streaming down her face, all down the hill from the Queen's Tomb and your man here chasing after her and pursuing her down into the trees! Yes!

AUDELLE. No!

FINGAL. Where God knows what happened.

AUDELLE. No!

FINGAL. You were seen!

AUDELLE. I swear to you. I swear before you all...

FINGAL *grabs his rifle and points it at* AUDELLE.

FINGAL. What? Ha? What?

BERKELEY. Fingal!

MRS GOULDING. Mr Fingal, how dare you?

FINGAL. Ah, ah. Now, nobody leaves till we get some answers.

MADELEINE. Mr Fingal...

FINGAL (*attaining a semblance of responsibility through his drunken fog*). You have nothing to fear, madam. I know this type. We will have an answer.

MADELEINE. Put the gun down, Mr Fingal, this instant.

FINGAL. No, do not presume to order me about! I haven't been paid in over a year, so I may as well take his brains with me on my way out. What have I got left anyhow? I don't care. You deflowered her, sir, didn't you?

AUDELLE. I did not.

FINGAL. You defiled her!

AUDELLE. I did not.

FINGAL. You have rendered her worthless.

AUDELLE. No, sir.

FINGAL. Well, I will shoot you dead, sir.

He points the barrel at AUDELLE*'s head.*

MRS GOULDING (*shouts*). Mr Fingal!

FINGAL. What?

Short pause.

MRS GOULDING. You are not well!

FINGAL. I am well enough.

BERKELEY *puts himself between* FINGAL *and* AUDELLE.

BERKELEY. Surely to God this is a misunderstanding!

Hannah…

HANNAH. That's not what happened, Mr Fingal.

FINGAL. Do not be afraid, Miss Hannah. There is no need for any lies now. This man does not deserve your protection.

AUDELLE. Hannah, please… Tell him…

HANNAH. Mr Fingal, I don't know who saw us, but they have misinterpreted what they saw.

FINGAL. You say I am a liar?

HANNAH. No!

FINGAL. But you say none of it happened?

HANNAH. Not in that way.

FINGAL. Then in what way? What way?

HANNAH. Mr Audelle asked if I might show him the Queen's
Tomb. There was still just enough light so we walked up the
path, up out of the glen and on up the side of Knockmullen...

Short pause.

FINGAL. Go on.

HANNAH. Mr Audelle went on ahead of me as I was fatigued.
When I reached the tomb I sat alone. After he had been out
of sight for some minutes I realised there was someone
sheltering within the mouth of the tomb, a man and a woman
who were watching me. I called out for Mr Audelle to show
them I wasn't alone. On hearing my voice, the figures in the
tomb stumbled out. And as they lurched towards me I
realised I was somehow seeing... myself and Mr Audelle! It
was us but... our corpses... walking. And I... I turned and
ran. I slipped and slid all the way back down to the road at
Knockmullen, until Mr Audelle caught up to me. I was
unable to tell him what had happened, as I scarcely know
myself, but that is the truth, Mr Fingal, and that is the event
which must have been witnessed and of which you have
heard. For myself, I said nothing.

MADELEINE. Oh, Hannah...

HANNAH. What could I say? I am so tired of all the trouble I
keep bringing on this house!

MADELEINE. You don't. You never do.

BERKELEY. The child saw some hungry souls sheltering in the
hollow. The gloaming and her imagination did the rest.
Indeed we are maybe thankful Mr Audelle was on hand, we
should thank him.

Pause.

FINGAL. You gave her that laudanum to drink, didn't you?

AUDELLE. No, I… I… (*Laughs.*)

MADELEINE. Laudanum?

FINGAL. Laudanum. And it has unbalanced the child.

MRS GOULDING. No, sir!

AUDELLE. No, no… It's merely a tincture I use as a cough suppressant.

MRS GOULDING. I know what laudanum is, Mr Audelle. You were trying to get Clare to procure it for you in Jamestown and I forbade it!

FINGAL. And me, like a bloody fool getting it for you.

MRS GOULDING. You got it for him?!

FINGAL. I didn't know the devil was going to give it to a child! A child!

AUDELLE. No! I meant no harm…

FINGAL. No harm? Look at her! Look at her!

BERKELEY. I'm sure Mr Audelle only wanted to help Hannah suppress her cough.

FINGAL (*disparaging*). Ah! Rather he wanted to render her senseless and have his way. I know that game!

HANNAH. No. I asked him for it. Yes, I took it, but I asked him for it!

MADELEINE. Oh, Hannah! Why?

HANNAH. Because I needed to see the future. And I did. I saw it. We performed a rite and I saw it!

MADELEINE. You performed a what?

BERKELEY. No, no… Not a rite.

HANNAH. We performed a rite in here. And I saw it.

MADELEINE. What do you mean, 'a rite'?

BERKELEY. No, no, no, no, no, no, no, not a rite. Some
prayers merely, a few words in order to...

FINGAL. Why don't you shut up, Reverend? I'm tired of
hearing your interminable voice, and I don't want to hear
another damn word out of you. I am in charge here tonight so
you can just shut up. And you too, Mrs Goulding.

MRS GOULDING. I never said a word!

FINGAL. Yes, well, don't.

MRS GOULDING. Yes, well, I didn't.

FINGAL. Yes, well, don't.

MRS GOULDING. Well, you have said enough. You gobaloon.

GRANDIE. Let her sing!

MRS GOULDING. Yes, shush, Grandie, shush now.

MADELEINE. Berkeley, you better tell me what you did or I'll
take this gun and shoot you myself.

HANNAH. No. I needed to understand what was happening to
me, Mama. But I know now I was seeing and hearing what is
yet to be! Not the past! I have never seen the past. I saw that
the child I have heard crying here is my child, the child I will
never know because I will perish bringing it into the world.

MADELEINE. No!

HANNAH. After I go to Northampton. Yes.

MADELEINE. Hannah, no...

HANNAH. Yes! And I saw that I would forever wander looking
for my baby. I have seen what eternity holds for me.

MADELEINE. No! This is preposterous!

HANNAH. I will be locked in a room. And that room is death
and there is no door from which to leave. I saw it all!

MADELEINE. No!

FINGAL. Right. (*To* AUDELLE.) You see what yous have done? You see it? You put the girl in a state like that, and you drive her insane? What possible purpose can you have? You have no purpose. No purpose but to defile and destroy and degrade. (*Aims the rifle to shoot* AUDELLE.) What conceivable good can your presence bring in the world?

BERKELEY. Wait, Fingal...

MADELEINE. Mr Fingal...

AUDELLE. No purpose.

Pause.

FINGAL. You brought this on yourself, Mr Audelle, for none can make sense of your actions.

HANNAH. Or your actions, Mr Fingal!

FINGAL. Ha?

HANNAH. I say what of your actions?

FINGAL. My actions?

HANNAH. You skulk in here and sit in judgement on all of us like the coward who can only hold his head up when he has a weapon. What do you know about fairness or rightness, you ignorant lout?

FINGAL. You dare to speak to me like that? You were always mad. All of yous always were. Look at your Grandie. She's never had a bloody clue what in the name of Jaysus is going on! Or your father? Who brought this whole place to its knees before hanging himself in front of his own child practically! Your cold-hearted mother there, hardly even of this earth so remote and incomprehensible are her secret wishes!

MADELEINE. You are drunk, Mr Fingal.

FINGAL. I'm not drunk. Nor was I drunk all those nights I was fetched up here to lock that mad bastard in a room upstairs while you and I sat here with the long hours ticking by.

MADELEINE. You are drunk, sir, and you will put that gun down this instant.

She goes to grab him. He pushes her away roughly.

BERKELEY. Fingal!

FINGAL. I don't care, do you hear me?! I've had it up to here with all of you. No longer will I walk out of this bloody house, ignorant of the forces that keep me perpetually on my knees! No longer!

MADELEINE. No, sir! You are drunk, sir! What ever will you think when you have come to your senses?

FINGAL. I am in my senses.

MADELEINE. Well, what do you want? What are you asking of us?

FINGAL (*drunkenly*). What?

HANNAH. Mr Fingal cannot bear to come to his senses for then he must face what he has done.

FINGAL. I'm in my senses, don't you worry about that.

HANNAH. Oh yes, and were you in your senses when you did what you did and went and beat James Furay? Have you seen him? (*Pause.*) Have you?!

MRS GOULDING. What happened to James Furay?

HANNAH. Tell them what you did.

Pause.

MADELEINE. What did he do?

FINGAL. No... I...

MRS GOULDING. Is he alright?

HANNAH. I have seen him, Mr Fingal. I went to say goodbye to him today. And I found him in the gate lodge. Yes. With no fire lit. No candle burning. I found him curled up in the cold of the loft, Mr Fingal, lying in his own mess of congealed blood and pus.

Pause.

FINGAL. Yes... well...

MRS GOULDING. What happened to him?

Pause.

What happened to him?

FINGAL (*quietly*). I beat him.

MRS GOULDING. What?

FINGAL. I beat him! I beat him!

MRS GOULDING. What did you beat him for?

FINGAL. I had to.

HANNAH. You had to? He couldn't get down the ladder from his bed by himself. He couldn't even look at me. He forbade me to fetch the doctor. He begged me not to tell anyone. I bathed his wounds which are so deep and vicious he will surely be marked for the rest of his life. I couldn't even bandage him for fear the cloth would only stick into his wounds causing him greater agony – and I knew I was supposed to be leaving here tomorrow!? We both wept there, Mr Fingal, each of us hiding their tears from the other. I, for the misery I was about to leave him in. But do you know why he wept? Out of shame, sir! For shame! That boy who was brought up as my brother, and was almost as much as your son! But you are not worthy of him, Mr Fingal. How can I go and marry a man I hardly know when I am unable to provide affection for those I truly love?! You have caused me to stay, Mr Fingal. Not Mr Audelle, not Berkeley or my mother, but you, sir! So do what you will and go home.

FINGAL *looks at them all.*

MADELEINE. Mr Fingal. Why would you do such a thing?

Pause.

FINGAL. For you.

MADELEINE. For me?

FINGAL. I wanted to show you I can be strong. I wanted to show you I can bring discipline to this place, and I'm not just some... joke.

MADELEINE. But, Mr Fingal...

FINGAL. You were so angry about the horses! You told me to put the boy before his responsibilities!

MADELEINE. But I would never have wanted you to beat him, Mr Fingal!

FINGAL. It was the morning after all the buildings collapsed! I'd been up the whole night, sitting up on my own, knowing how bad things were going to get now. You never think how hard it is for me. To have to show my face in Jamestown! Even my own family are ashamed of me! They hate me all round the country all around here because of my loyalty to you. No one respects me. But I stay. I stay. And I stay because I am faithful to you – (*Short pause, he looks at the floor.*) and because I've always loved you! I can't help it! You don't know how hard I've tried to ignore it. To banish it! But then once again your eyes fall on me and my heart submits. It's never stopped. It's beyond my abilities. I walk around with no money in my pockets, it doesn't matter, the locals and their keepers laugh at me, it doesn't matter. I see your face in my mind and it just doesn't matter because I know I would live in a moment forever if you might just deign to put out your hand to me. Even if it were my last moment on this earth. Don't you see that? Of course you do. You have seen it. You know it. But what do you do? You use it. You use it to keep me, and use me. And you know what? I don't care, do you see? I don't care because I still love you! (*Pause. Looks at them all.*) It's all just a big trick though, really, I suppose, isn't it? It's just a big joke that keeps us all running around in God's playground for his amusement. And we all think it's so real…

Pause. FINGAL *is drowning in his own confusion. He has ended up on the floor near* MADELEINE. *She reaches out, touches his face tenderly then brings her lips to his. They kiss for a moment and then lay their heads together, their foreheads touching.*

BERKELEY. Well… There now, my good man. That's alright.

BERKELEY *goes to* FINGAL *and takes the gun from him gently.*

We are all overwrought. Yes. That's alright. A little drink of water.

He hands the gun to CLARE *behind* FINGAL*'s back. She takes it out to the hall quietly and comes back to stand in the doorway.*

Mrs Goulding.

MRS GOULDING. Yes, of course.

She pours some water to bring to BEREKLEY.

BERKELEY. There's a good man. Let us walk out to the steps and get us some fresh air, shall we? Yes…

BERKELEY *signals for* MRS GOULDING *to open the doors to the conservatory, which she does.* BERKELEY *leads* FINGAL *towards the conservatory.* FINGAL *turns to the room.*

FINGAL. I'm… I'm sorry.

BERKELEY. That's alright. Come on now, there's a good man.

BERKELEY *brings* FINGAL *out through the conservatory.*

MADELEINE. Are you alright, Mr Audelle?

AUDELLE. Yes.

MRS GOULDING. I don't know what has come over him. He has lost his mind completely. Here, Mr Audelle, sit down, take a drink.

AUDELLE. Thank you.

MRS GOULDING. And Grandie. Poor Grandie.

AUDELLE. Is she alright?

MADELEINE. She'll be fine.

MRS GOULDING *gets them some drinks.*

Are you alright, Clare?

CLARE. Yes, ma'am.

MADELEINE. You are gone quite pale. Will you sit by the fire?

CLARE. No thank you, ma'am.

MADELEINE. Are you sure?

CLARE. Yes, ma'am.

Pause.

MRS GOULDING. Yes, well. I will make a bread poultice to bring down to James Furay.

MADELEINE. But bring him up to stay here tonight, please, Mrs Goulding.

MRS GOULDING. Yes, madam.

MADELEINE. Can we light some more candles please?

MRS GOULDING. We will, of course. Clare, come and help me light the house.

CLARE. Yes, ma'am.

MRS GOULDING *and* CLARE *leave. Pause.*

HANNAH. I'm sorry, Mama.

MADELEINE. No.

AUDELLE. Do not fear your future, Miss Hannah. A child you cannot save, being locked in a room from which you cannot escape. That is not your future, I can assure you.

HANNAH. How so?

AUDELLE. Because you saw my present, not your future. The locked room is this moment I may never escape from. The child you hear crying is the ever waking dream child whose sobs I dose myself to quiet. She is the child I abandoned. Such is your gift, you saw Hell, Miss Hannah. But it was my hell. The nightmare unto which each morning delivers me and each evening awakens me to contemplate. Do not fear your future. It is as open as the sky. I must ask you ladies to forgive me. I must administer my medicine.

AUDELLE *bows to them and goes out.*

GRANDIE (*listening*). The old dog.

MADELEINE. Are you alright, Grandie?

GRANDIE. The blind old dog used live here long ago.

MADELEINE. What of him?

GRANDIE. Can you hear him? Barking?

Pause. There is a sudden deafening bang in the hallway which shakes the whole house. They are startled into silence.

MADELEINE. What is it?

HANNAH *steps towards the hallway door.* BERKELEY *comes in through the conservatory doors holding a candle, as smoke drifts in from the hallway.*

BERKELEY. Did you hear it? Did you hear it again?

Offstage, we hear CLARE *scream and run down the stairs.* HANNAH *stands looking into the hallway, her hands up to her face.* CLARE *comes in.*

CLARE. It's Mr Audelle! (*Short pause.*) He got the rifle!

BERKELEY. Where is he?

CLARE. He's in the hallway! (*Turns and goes out.*) Oh, Mrs Goulding! Mrs Goulding!

The lights change as everyone but GRANDIE *drifts out to the hallway. An afternoon materialises around* GRANDIE *as she sits there. It is two weeks later, Friday June 7th.* FINGAL *comes in, puts some hardbacked ledgers on the table and stands waiting, much as he did in the first scene of the play. He wears a new dark coat with brass buttons. His hair is brushed across his head and his black eye is healed.* MRS GOULDING *comes into the room with a shawl round her shoulders.*

MRS GOULDING. Well, Mr Fingal.

FINGAL. Mrs Goulding.

MRS GOULDING. Your arrangements are all made?

FINGAL. Yes. We leave tonight.

MRS GOULDING. Yes?

FINGAL. We'll be married in Swords in County Dublin and sail for Liverpool next Tuesday morning.

MRS GOULDING. When do you leave for Canada?

FINGAL. In the following week. Clare's sister will house us.

MRS GOULDING. Very good. Clare is a clever girl.

FINGAL. I know.

MRS GOULDING. Well, look after her. (*Pause.*) She is your salvation, Mr Fingal.

FINGAL. I have left a copy of the accounts here for madam.

MRS GOULDING. Yes, she will be into you herself in a moment. The Colonel is delayed. You heard he shot at some intruders last night.

FINGAL. Yes, I heard. (*Short pause*.) Is it true you will be kept on?

MRS GOULDING. Yes, the Colonel has asked me personally to keep the house for his daughter. James Furay will remain in the gate lodge and act as groundsman to the estate.

FINGAL. Well, that's... He'll make an excellent groundsman.

Pause.

MRS GOULDING. Yes, well, I wish you luck, sir.

FINGAL. Thank you.

She shakes his hand. MADELEINE *comes in*.

MRS GOULDING. Would Grandie like some tea? I think she would. Are you warm enough there, Grandie?

She goes and settles some cushions around GRANDIE.

I'll bring us up some nice soup, will I?

MADELEINE. Thank you, Mrs Goulding.

MRS GOULDING. Yes, not at all.

She leaves.

MADELEINE. Are these the accounts?

FINGAL. Yes, madam, in order of year, most recent on top.

MADELEINE. Grim reading no doubt. Have you received your money?

FINGAL. Yes. Thank you. (*Hands her a small bag with some coins in it*.) I wondered if I might give you this to pass on to James Furay for me. I haven't had a chance to... to see him.

MADELEINE. That's very generous. I'm sure he will be most grateful. You have enough for your passage?

FINGAL. Yes, we'll be fine.

MADELEINE. Well, congratulations.

FINGAL. Thank you.

MADELEINE. When is the wedding?

FINGAL. Next Monday. In Swords, in County Dublin. A relative of Clare's knows the curate there. We sail for Liverpool on Tuesday.

MADELEINE. I'm very pleased for you both.

Pause.

FINGAL. I trust Miss Hannah is in good health.

MADELEINE. Yes, I had a letter from her just this morning. She is arrived in Northampton. All is well. As soon as I have settled my affairs here with Colonel Bennett, myself and Grandie shall join her.

FINGAL. Well, please send her my congratulations and I wish you all the very best.

MADELEINE. Thank you.

FINGAL. Right, well. (*Gathers himself to leave but halts near the door.*) Madeleine.

MRS GOULDING *returns.*

MRS GOULDING. Madam, a boy came to the door and says the Colonel will be here in thirty minutes. They are inspecting the back gate.

MADAM. Thank you, Mrs Goulding.

MRS GOULDING. Is it chilly? Will I light the fire?

MRS GOULDING *goes to the fireplace and rakes it with the poker.*

MADELEINE. Light it for Grandie. I don't particularly want to encourage the Colonel to stay. Bring some tea for him in the small parlour and we may conduct our business in there.

MRS GOULDING. Very good. I haven't forgotten you, Grandie. Wrap up there, we'll light this for you in a minute and I'll be back with hot soup in the flea's time.

FINGAL. Right. Well, I'll… Goodbye.

MADELEINE. Goodbye, Mr Fingal. Thank you.

FINGAL. Goodbye.

MRS GOULDING. Goodbye, Mr Fingal.

FINGAL. Goodbye.

He leaves. Pause.

MRS GOULDING. Right.

MADELEINE. Thank you, Mrs Goulding.

MRS GOULDING (*tone of 'That's that…'*). Now…

She leaves.

MADELEINE *looks out the window then starts to peruse the ledgers.*

GRANDIE. A boy once proposed to me who was from Northampton, but Daddy wouldn't brook it. He had a kind face. He wasn't good-looking but he was kind. It will be nice to be near him. Won't it?

MADELEINE (*absently*). Yes, it will be nice for all of us, won't it?

GRANDIE. Yes.

(S*ings*.)
    While the green moss grows
    Upon the heather
    Where the briar grows
    Upon the wood…

That's their song. Madeleine.

MADELEINE. Whose song, Grandie?

GRANDIE. The old people.

MADELEINE (*absently, making a note*). Yes?

GRANDIE. Yes. The hunters. They were here. Before the
farmers came. Oh, thousands of years ago, Madeleine.
Before you were born! Before you or I owned this land. But
nobody really owns it, of course. It owns us. Did I ever tell
you I once met a man out there under the trees who had
mirrors where his eyes should be?

MADELEINE (*working*). No, I don't think so.

GRANDIE. Oh yes. He was some kind of king, apparently. He
told me all about it. About the people who were here before.
And he taught me that old song.

MADELEINE. Who did?

GRANDIE. The king I met who had mirror eyes. I met him out
there on the path one morning just as it was getting bright,
and he told me all about the people who lived here thousands
of years ago. Thousands of years before St Patrick even.
Before anyone. The very first people who lived here. They
used to hunt in the forest and they caught fish in little boats
down off the shore. They were very gentle people, he told
me. But then different people came you see. They came up
over the sea from the south. They were farmers. They had a
different god and they came here and they chopped down the
trees so they could graze their cattle and do you know what
they did? They killed all the hunters! Yes! They made big
tombs, and they burnt all the hunters' families and they put
them in there so their gods would protect them from the
hunters, because they were still afraid of them, even after
they had killed them.

MADELEINE. What farmers?

GRANDIE. The farmers who came here and killed all the
hunters in the forest. The hunters were a gentle people.
Some called them the good people, and some called them
the old people and some called them something else. But

the mirror-eyed king, that I met out there, he said the real
reason we can't forget them is because our gods actually
bow before their gods. Apparently. Now. What about that?
You always look after me so well, Madeleine. Don't think I
don't know.

MADELEINE. What's that?

GRANDIE. I say even when I don't know who is here or how
old I am, I always feel safe when I see you.

MADELEINE. Well, that's good, isn't it?

GRANDIE. Yes. You are a good mother, Madeleine.

MADELEINE. Am I?

GRANDIE. You don't mind?

MADELEINE (*smiles*). How could I mind?

GRANDIE *shrugs*.

Of course I don't mind!

BERKELEY *comes in. He looks a bit sleepy. He wears a
woollen cardigan.*

Oh, hello, did you have a good sleep?

BERKELEY. Yes. Too good. Have I missed the Colonel?

MADELEINE. No, he was delayed. Did you hear he shot at
some intruders on his estate last night?

BERKELEY. No!

MADELEINE. Yes, well, he's on his way.

BERKELEY. Intruders!

MADELEINE. Yes.

BERKELEY. Right. Oh dear, well… I thought I should say
hello.

MADELEINE. We received a letter from Northampton this morning. Hannah has arrived.

BERKELEY. Oh, that is good news. And… she is well?

MADELEINE. She slept soundly, remarking on the peculiar silence of the estate.

BERKELEY (*concurring*). Yes.

MADELEINE *brings him the letter*.

MADELEINE. Lord Ashby sends you his personal condolences about Mr Audelle.

MADELEINE *goes back to her work*.

BERKELEY. How kind. (*Glancing over the letter.*) I had the strangest dreams. I woke up feeling quite anxious, I must say. You do think we are doing the right thing, Madeleine? Leaving Audelle here? When we go to Northampton?

MADELEINE. Oh yes. I should think he likes it here, Berkeley. The graveyard is so quiet and such a peaceful place to rest. And I know the Colonel would never mind you paying your respects when we return on a visit. Leave him here, Berkeley.

BERKELEY. Yes, I know. You are right. I just… I mean, I was his family.

MADELEINE. Of course. And you were very good to him, Berkeley. (*Short pause.*) Now, Mrs Goulding is bringing some soup up for Grandie. Will you have some? You will.

BERKELEY. Yes, Madeleine. Thank you.

MADELEINE. Good. (*Looks out the window.*) Oh. Will you sit with Grandie for a few minutes, Berkeley?

BERKELEY. Of course I will.

MADELEINE *picks up the ledgers and makes to leave*.

Good luck.

MADELEINE. Thanks.

BERKELEY. I know you will charm a price way over the odds from him.

MADELEINE. Oh, stop it now.

BERKELEY. Will you tell the Colonel I must say hello before he goes?

MADELEINE. I will.

BERKELEY. Madeleine?

She halts at the door.

I… appreciate your… understanding.

MADELEINE. What's to understand?

She leaves. BERKELEY *opens the letter and brings it to the window for better light.*

BERKELEY. Well, Grandie, we'll all be going soon now, won't we?

GRANDIE. Yes.

BERKELEY. We'll all ride a cock horse to Banbury Cross. And delicious soup on the way. We are such lucky souls are we not?

GRANDIE. We are, yes!

GRANDIE *sings softly, almost silently, to herself while she goes to the mantelpiece. She gently touches some of the ornaments there, glancing at herself in the mirror.* MRS GOULDING *brings in a tray with some bowls, and lays the table for their lunch, then leaves to fetch the food.* BERKELEY *stands in the window, absorbed in the letter with his hand to his face.* GRANDIE's *singing fades to silence while she stands looking high into the mirror.* BERKELEY'S *attention is drawn from his letter. He observes* GRANDIE *as the lights gradually fade.*

End.